LONG ISLAND
FOOD

LONG ISLAND
FOOD

A HISTORY FROM FAMILY FARMS &
OYSTERS TO CRAFT SPIRITS

T.W. BARRITT

AMERICAN PALATE

Published by American Palate

A Division of The History Press

Charleston, SC 29403

www.historypress.net

Cover images, front cover: oyster image by Jacob Skoglund; barn and eggs image by T.W. Barritt.
Back cover: oystermen image by Richard Bowditch; octopus plate image by Jacob Skoglund.

First published 2015

Manufactured in the United States

ISBN 978.1.62619.846.3

Library of Congress Control Number: 2015944410

Contents

Acknowledgements

Much like the evolution of Long Island food, this book is the culmination of a journey, with many stops and side trips along the way. I want to thank my parents, Dorothy and Jim Barritt, who taught me to cook and inspired me to explore Long Island at an early age.

I must thank all the people who are shaping the future of Long Island food and who were so generous with their time in sharing their stories with me. I am in awe of the work that you do. You are writing the story of Long Island food each day, and this book is dedicated to you.

There were many people who were instrumental in bringing this volume to life. Whitney Landis and The History Press found me and asked me to consider taking on the significant challenge of chronicling the story of Long Island food. Special thanks go to Jacob Skoglund, who provided first-rate support as image curator and photographer for the project.

Many thanks and much appreciation go to the talented photographers whose excellent work illustrates this story: John Barritt, Richard Bowditch, Lucia Cascio, Randee Daddona, Adrian Fanning, Ana Miyares and Jacob Skoglund.

There were many people who offered their guidance and support. Thanks to Kathy Curran and Wendy Palhernus-Annibell at the Suffolk County Historical Society. Much appreciation goes to Lydia Walshin, Jane Lottes and Monica Marshall for their wise counsel; Matthew Kalamidas for his photo image advice; and Steve Price for his superhuman editing and proofreading skills. Special thanks to Laura "Lucky" Luciano, who was generous in making introductions.

Thanks go to the faithful readers of my blog, "Culinary Types," who first showed an interest in the stories I shared about Long Island food, and to Betsy Davidson and Eileen Duffy of *Edible Long Island* and *Edible East End*, who encourage me to continue to explore and tell stories about what Long Islanders eat.

Finally, I must give a nod to my friend and colleague Splint McCullough, who was present the day my plan to write about food first took shape and who has provided me with endless material and encouragement ever since.

Prologue

Long Island Food

A Work in Progress

I was well into my teenage years before I realized that there was more to food than TV dinners. I'm ashamed to admit that I considered the TV dinner to be an epicurean wonder. It was my ethnic food. The perfect aluminum packaging, the geometric sections that held each food item and the very idea that the main course and the dessert could exist side by side inspired endless fascination. The fact that we could enjoy our piping-hot turkey with gravy, whipped mashed potatoes, sweet peas and apple cobbler while watching an episode of *Bewitched* was just the icing on the cake. Clearly, I had a limited frame of reference when it came to food.

I grew up on suburban Long Island in the 1960s. Life was catapulting toward the space age. New home construction was booming. Convenience and economics drove food purchases. A young mother with four boys needed meal options that were affordable and easy to assemble. It was all about feeding the family three square meals a day. White bread, Jell-O and tuna casserole—that's what I remember. Our idea of haute cuisine was pigs-in-a-blanket. A cone of Carvel soft-serve vanilla ice cream with sprinkles—enjoyed lustfully in the back seat of a Ford station wagon—was a real treat.

We never thought of Long Island as a food haven. I began to develop a sense of place in Mrs. Zulauf's third-grade class. Our history text was a chronology of Long Island people and events. We learned that Native Americans had once occupied our suburban plots of land and that windmills had dotted the East End of Long Island, but there was no mention of a distinctive cuisine.

The idea of a Long Island food culture was really not so outlandish. There were hints along the way. We lived a short distance from the local agricultural college located in a town called Farmingdale.

Even in the suburban neighborhood of my youth, farming was happening right across the street (although we likely considered it large-scale gardening). Our neighbors, Rose and Vincenzo Maio, had emigrated from Italy and settled in Massapequa in the early 1950s. They had constructed their home by hand on a plot of land that consisted of about one-quarter of a generous suburban block. Mr. and Mrs. Maio worked the land every day of the year. They raised lettuce, escarole, garlic, zucchini, potatoes, string beans and tomatoes. They cultivated fragrant herbs for cooking such as bay leaves, dill, parsley and basil. The property contained apple trees, pear trees, peach trees, fig trees and grapevines.

The Maios lived frugally. Mrs. Maio canned the fruits and vegetables they harvested. She also propagated plants, flowers and vegetables from the previous year's seeds. Today, we call that "sustainability." The Maios' small "farm" would rival the size and scope of many modern Community Sponsored Agriculture (CSA) projects on Long Island, designed to feed multiple families.

Mr. and Mrs. Maio's story was really no different than those of the first settlers who came to Long Island. Most don't realize that when originally settled more than three centuries ago, Long Island was a thriving agrarian society. Long Island's first European transplants were not professional farmers but property owners who learned gradually to support themselves using the natural resources around them.

The story of Long Island food is one of past, present and future. It is a stew of many flavors—ethnic diversity, commerce and economy, industrialization, convenience, tradition—and today a new food sensibility that draws on all of those ingredients and more.

Here are some basic statistics about Long Island. Shaped like a fish with two fins and surrounded by water, Long Island is 118 miles long and 20 miles wide. Formed by a glacier more than six thousand years ago, it is the longest contiguous island in the United States. When we talk about Long Island, we mean the counties of Nassau and Suffolk, which cover central and eastern Long Island. Technically, the boroughs of Brooklyn and Queens are part of the same geographical package, but they are not considered Long Island in the colloquial sense.

The essentials of Long Island food haven't changed much since Native Americans occupied the land. This is an island where fishing, farming and livestock flourished. Native Americans called Long Island *Paumanok*, or "land of tribute." Other evidence suggests that the Algonquian word *Sewanhacky* ("place of shells") was the first name for Long Island. Tradition holds that there were thirteen Native American tribes living on Long Island in the mid-1600s when European settlers began to arrive, although the accuracy of that claim has been challenged in recent years. We do know that Native Americans who inhabited Long Island were hunters and fishermen. They ate venison, bear, raccoon, turkey, quail, partridge, goose and duck. Some farmed, cultivating crops of beans and corn. They ground corn with a mortar and pestle and cooked a dish called "samp," a thick porridge of corn, beans and preserved meat. They also harvested oysters, clams and fish from the salt waters that surround Long Island.

As European settlers populated the region, the Dutch settled to the west and the English settled to the east. They farmed, but they also brought their own food traditions, as immigrants did in the centuries that followed.

Modern-day Long Island is a land of many personalities and contradictions. Infuriating traffic, suburban sprawl and congestion is juxtaposed against serene beauty. You'll encounter tract housing and Gold Coast mansions, big-box stores and lush vineyards, strip malls and seashores, food courts and farms. It's sometimes hard to put a finger on which Long Island is the genuine article, and it is challenging to put a label on Long Island food. There is no rigid recipe, and the area is not known for one food or culinary tradition. A single landmass, it is a diverse mix of foodstuffs, cultures and historic traditions.

We live in a society where food is celebrated as an art form—perhaps to excess—but there are far more practical reasons that characterize the food of a region, such as basic economic realities and the need for sustenance. If Long Island food culture is one big pot of stew, there are six ingredients that create its distinctive character and flavor. Keep these in mind when reading the stories collected in this volume:

- FEEDING THE FAMILY: Long Island was settled as an agrarian society where the first priority for the head of the household was to put food on the family table.

- FARMING AND MARITIME RESOURCES: Long Island offered Native Americans and European settlers abundant food options harvested from the soil and the ocean.

- ETHNIC TRADITIONS: Immigrants who entered America through the port of New York and settled on Long Island brought with them agricultural and livestock trades, food preferences and customs still evident today.

- LOCATION: Long Island's proximity to New York City fueled the local economy and influenced the choice and volume of food products that were produced here and transported to urban areas.

- PATTERNS OF GROWTH, DECLINE AND REINVENTION: Seminal Long Island food products and businesses experienced significant periods of prosperity, but in time, environmental and economic challenges precipitated declines and forced purveyors to either shutter or find ways to reimagine their businesses.

- SENSE OF PLACE: Long Island's local food identity is defined by everything from broad marketing opportunities to personal passions.

As I became more food aware, I was envious of my friends who lived near well-established foodie destinations—places like California's Napa Valley, Virginia's Rappahannock County and New York's Hudson Valley. Their hometown pride was valid and somewhat annoying, as well. I felt that in the fight for foodie bragging rights, I was facing a losing battle. So I started to explore and discovered that a food revival was happening all around me—one that had historic precedent. Long Island was reaching back to its agricultural and maritime roots as it worked to cultivate a new food culture.

It's easy to stick to the highway and yield to the temptation to pick up your food at the drive-thru window, but if you do, you will miss out. Wander off the Long Island Expressway and you will discover a world of surprises—heirloom tomatoes, oysters, laying hens hidden in suburban enclaves, hydroponic lettuce, goat cheese, micro-greens, sparkling wine and hard cider. Long Island food is experiencing a renaissance.

This is the story of Long Island's historic connection to food. More importantly, it is the story of today's pioneers, craftsmen and artisans who are forging a new food culture on Long Island. As a journalist and food blogger, I gain insights from the stories of individuals. What is history but a collection of stories about individuals and their accomplishments? It would be impossible to gather all of the stories that define Long Island food, but within these pages you will meet some of the individuals who are forging a new tradition. They are farmers, cheese makers, chefs, brewers, bakers and entrepreneurs. They are the new curators of Long Island's food history, and they are advancing our food culture with a healthy respect for the past as they put their own imprint on our next chapter. Through them, we can learn what once transpired and guess what may emerge in the future in terms of how and what we eat. In the twenty-first century, Long Island is a place where you can harvest heirloom tomatoes on a suburban farm, sweeten your yogurt with local honey or sip craft vodka made from local potatoes. Yes, we're evolving beyond casseroles, but we haven't abandoned our love of comfort food either. There's always time for a juicy burger and shake or a plate piled high with fried soft-shell clams.

Chapter 1
Farming

Then and Now

Anyone who grew up on Long Island in the mid- to late twentieth century knows that life here revolves around the family. The word *family* precedes an unusual number of words in Long Island's popular lexicon. There are "family dinners," "family-style restaurants," "family-owned businesses," "family movies" and so on. The postwar suburban building boom almost guaranteed that on Long Island, the nuclear family would be considered the primary societal unit.

At the heart of Long Island food is the family farm, although if you were to survey the average man or woman on the street, they'd probably have no clue about Long Island's farming heritage. Farming seems so old-fashioned in this high-tech world, and sadly, so much evidence of our farming society has been paved over—literally. However, when European settlers first populated Long Island in the early seventeenth century, their primary objective was to feed the family.

"The East End was settled by the English, and the western region was settled by the Dutch, close to New York City," said Joseph Gergela, former executive director of the nonprofit Long Island Farm Bureau and a retired third-generation Long Island farmer. "They were basically self-sustaining agrarian societies back then, cohabitating with the Indians."

Heads of households were not professional farmers but rather family providers. Everything a family needed to survive was planted, cultivated and harvested from the land. Many of those first Long Island families—descended from original settlers—have farmed for generations. Their family names are still evident today on everything from street signs to businesses to townships—names such as Hallock, Harbes, Corwin, Horton, Grossmann, Lewin, Wickham, Schmidt, Terry and so many more. Although so much erstwhile farmland has been replaced by suburban sprawl, highways and strip malls, the spirits of our founding farm families certainly linger on.

Climate and soil were accommodating to those first farm families. Surrounded by ocean water that warmed the land and kept temperatures moderate, they experienced a longer growing season. They learned to work with the unique characteristics of the well-drained soil.

"Long Island is the result of a glacier, and we were very blessed with sandy loam soils," said Gergela. "They're not very rich with organic material, so we've always had to use enhancements, and even in colonial days, they used fish as fertilizer to grow crops."

As British rule extended throughout the region in the late seventeenth century, there was an attempt to create a class of landed gentry, offering large land grants to wealthy families. Manor houses were created, and the manor lords were empowered to collect taxes from families who farmed the land. Evidence of the manor system can be seen today at several locations. The Manor of St. George in Shirley was established in 1693 and originally included most of modern-day Brookhaven. Sylvester Manor on Shelter Island was built in 1652 and operated as a plantation. Today, it is a historic site and a working farm offering a Community Sponsored Agriculture (CSA) program that feeds more than one hundred families. Gergela noted that some of the manors grew supplies—such as vegetables, potatoes and dairy products—for the slave trade. "They would load up the boats and go down to the Caribbean to provide the slave trade with provisions. In exchange, they would bring back molasses, rum and sugar cane."

The manor system was not popular among colonists, and independent-minded settlers moved to areas where they could actually own property. After the American Revolution, the manor system became outmoded, but it was perhaps an early forerunner of how Long Island farmers would expand their operations and begin to feed the surrounding region.

Perhaps because it emerged out of family farming, Long Island agriculture was characterized by variety. "We had everything from A to Z and still do," explained Gergela. "Everything from asparagus to zucchini and everything in between." Irish, German and Polish immigrants grew "ethnic crops"—such as potatoes and cauliflower—which they had farmed for generations back home.

Improved methods of transportation influenced the amount of food and the types of crops grown. The Long Island Railroad began moving east in

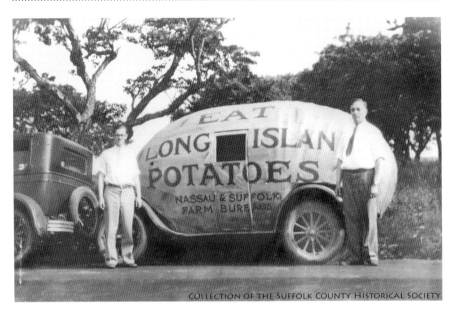

Long Island potato promotion: "Eat Long Island Potatoes: Nassau & Suffolk Farm Bureaus." Undated. *Copyright © Collection of the Suffolk County Historical Society.*

1834, linking small towns to New York City. City dwellers had great need for provisions, and the railroad afforded farmers an easy way to ship produce to New York City. Still, for a time, Long Island's largest crop was corded firewood, which city folks needed to keep their apartments heated.

The rise of the railroad coincided with an increase in production of storage crops that traveled well and would last for longer periods. Cabbage, cauliflower and potatoes became some of Long Island's biggest cash crops and helped cultivate the rise of the professional farmer, who now relied on newly developed farming equipment to increase his yield. Production of the renowned Long Island potato reached its height in the late 1940s with more than seventy thousand acres cultivated by more than one thousand farmers.

Long Island's open spaces were ideal for larger farming operations. Following the Civil War, immigrant farmers established "truck farms" that grew vegetables in large quantities that were trucked to nearby auction markets or directly into New York City. German farmers tended the Hempstead Plains. The Massapequa Farm District in Nassau County is now a busy area of asphalt, shopping centers and well-kept suburban dwellings. From the mid-1800s to the 1950s, immigrant farmers from Germany, Italy and eastern Europe and even a Chinese family raised vegetables and fruit as well as asters and dahlias for the New York City flower market.

Following World War II, Long Island faced a dilemma: where to house former servicemen and their families? A housing boom completely changed the shape and scope of agriculture on Long Island. Developers paid top price for farmland, and farmers cashed in. Their land was more valuable as real estate than for crop production. Over time, Nassau became a suburb of New York City, and agriculture became concentrated on the eastern end of Suffolk County.

Along the way, Long Island farmers adopted many products, and we made them our own. The Long Island potato and Long Island duckling gained fame far beyond Nassau and Suffolk Counties. The Green Newton Pippin Apple dates to 1730 and was first cultivated in Elmhurst, Queens. The Long Island cheese pumpkin took a very different journey to achieving heirloom status. The so-called pumpkin—which is considered by many the best option around for holiday pie filling—is actually a moschata squash, one of the oldest varieties of squashes cultivated. Ken Ettlinger, a founder of the Long Island Seed Project, noticed in the 1970s that the squash was becoming scarce. He started saving the seeds from moschata squash purchased from Long Island farmers and began marketing seeds for a "Long Island Cheese Pumpkin" through a company called the Long Island Seed Company. The

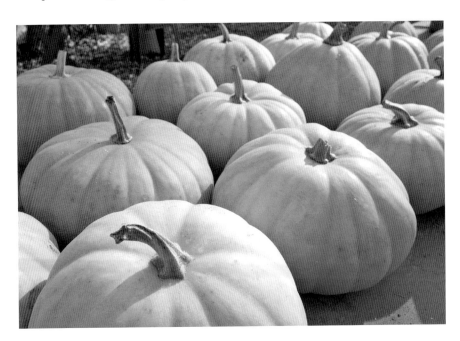

Long Island cheese pumpkins grown from heirloom seeds. *Photo by T.W. Barritt.*

name stuck, and what is now our hometown pumpkin is a favorite at farm stands and CSA programs each autumn.

Some professional family farmers have persevered, but their numbers have declined dramatically. Some have retired and some have sold land off to developers, but the most resilient have come up with new ways to keep farms afloat. They are nothing if not adaptable and respond bravely to everything from skyrocketing prices to changing demographics and consumer preferences—even to hurricanes and other damaging forces of nature.

Once the leading county for agriculture in New York State, Suffolk County has surrendered that top spot to Wyoming County and Cayuga County in upstate New York, which have increased their output due to production of dairy and Greek-style yogurt products. Most recent federal data lists the market value of farm goods produced in Suffolk County as $234 million between 2007 and 2012.

At the same time, there are various efforts underway to preserve agriculture as a way of life on Long Island. In 1974, Suffolk County initiated a Farmland Development Rights Program. A farmer can sell the development rights for his or her farmland to the county and receive a fair price for the land. The farmer still owns the land and must ensure that the property is only used for agricultural purposes. Since the program began, Suffolk County has protected more than ten thousand acres.

Public awareness of local farmers is increasing. Some grocery chains have taken to featuring the names and photos of local family farm suppliers in their weekly circulars. In December 2014, Riverhead Town received a state grant of $700,000 to create an agritourism center that would showcase the agriculture of the region and offer educational programs and tours to visitors.

As public concern over industrial farming practices escalate and families begin to value more mindful eating practices over volume and convenience, perceptions about food are changing. New farming models are emerging to feed Long Islanders. Community Sponsored Agriculture programs are increasing and working to invest residents more deeply in farming and methods for preparing locally grown food. Rare and colorful heirloom vegetable varieties are returning to our dinner plates thanks to the efforts of farmers looking to engage consumers' eyes and appetites. Organizations are evaluating how land is used. Historic land is being reclaimed for farming, and efforts are underway to preserve and celebrate Long Island's farming legacy through renovation of specific farm properties. Despite extraordinary suburban growth, Long Island still hosts an annual agricultural fair. Tilling the field is no longer just

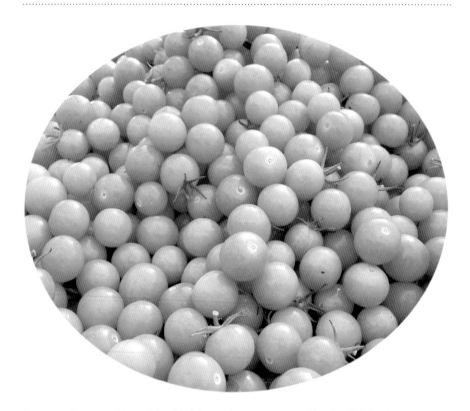

A summer harvest of Long Island heirloom cherry tomatoes. *Photo by T.W. Barritt.*

the purview of the professional farmer. Houses of worship, such as St. Francis Episcopal Church in North Bellmore, have turned underutilized lawns into extensive organic gardens that feed the growing numbers of hungry families on Long Island with fresh organic produce. Some organizations are even designing farming programs that nurture the body and the mind beyond basic daily nourishment.

RESTORATION FARM

It had been more than half a century since the land had been tilled at the Joshua Powell Farm in Old Bethpage when Caroline Fanning and Dan Holmes signed a lease to develop a Community Sponsored Agriculture program on the site. The 165-acre Powell farm was part of the Bethpage Purchase, a tract of land that European settler Thomas Powell purchased from three Native

American tribes in 1695. For nearly 150 years, Thomas Powell's descendants farmed the land as a small agrarian community. The Joshua Powell House—built by a descendant in the mid-1800s—still stands today. It is a centerpiece of Old Bethpage Village Restoration, a living-history museum of nineteenth-century structures relocated from all over Long Island. The Powell house is the only original structure on the museum property.

In 2007, Nassau County solicited bids to establish a working farm on the property as part of a "Healthy Nassau" campaign. Fanning and Holmes had been involved in a number of farming ventures on Long Island and in the Hudson Valley and were looking for an opportunity to establish a farm of their own. The county accepted their bid—one of two submitted—for a multiyear lease. "We knew it was going to be a viable farm just because it always had been," said Fanning. "It wasn't like being given five acres of asphalt with the promise of a load of compost to come in."

Fanning and Holmes were agricultural pioneers of a new kind on Long Island. At the time, the concept of Community Sponsored Agriculture—where community members purchase "a share" of risk or reward in the farm—was in its infancy in central Nassau County. The couple invested $50,000 of their savings to purchase tractors and began to plan the seven-acre patchwork of land plots. The first year, they often worked alone in the fields and started a farm stand at Old Bethpage Village Restoration to establish an initial presence with community members. "Call it youthful blindness," said Fanning. "We really didn't have a long-term vision other than just getting it off the ground."

Fanning hit the pavement to recruit members for the 2008 season, handing out brochures door to door and speaking at a local chamber of commerce meeting. The community responded enthusiastically. "It's a big leap of faith to put up $400 to a stranger without a track record, but we ended up selling all of our shares before the first season harvest began," she said.

In a time when fences often divide neighbors, the fields and open spaces of Restoration Farm invite people to connect with the land and Long Island's agrarian heritage in a working mid-nineteenth-century village where past meets present. The proximity to the original Powell farm means that members are treated to sweeping views of pastures, cows and sheep and historic homes from pre–Civil War Long Island. Seeing costumed interpreters from the living-history museum passing by the fields, it is not unusual to wonder if you've been transported back in time.

Now married with two children, Fanning and Holmes have redefined the notion of the "family farm" as Joshua Powell would have known it. Restoration

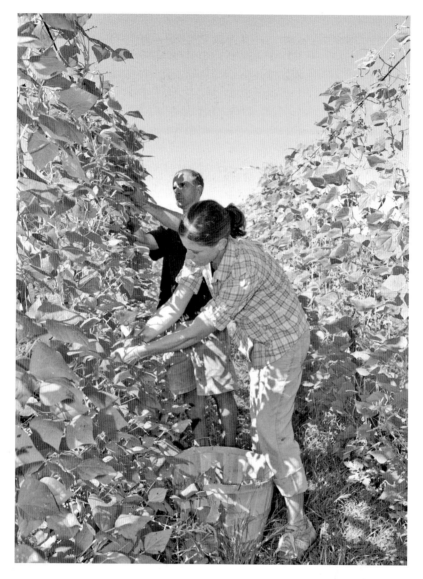

Head growers Dan Holmes and Caroline Fanning harvest at Restoration Farm.
Photo courtesy Adrian Fanning.

Farm provides fresh produce weekly to 150 households. Members of the Fanning and Holmes families work daily as volunteers, including Fanning's grandfather George Garbarini, who is in his mid-eighties.

The farm follows principles of sustainable agriculture, using no herbicides, pesticides or synthetic fertilizer, and practices crop rotation and

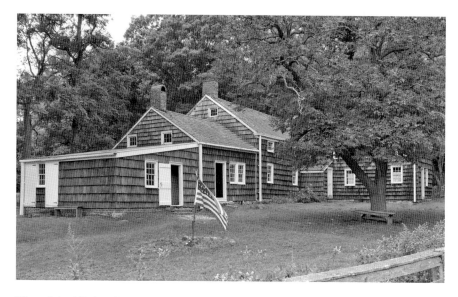

The original Joshua Powell farmhouse at Old Bethpage Village Restoration. *Photo by T.W. Barritt.*

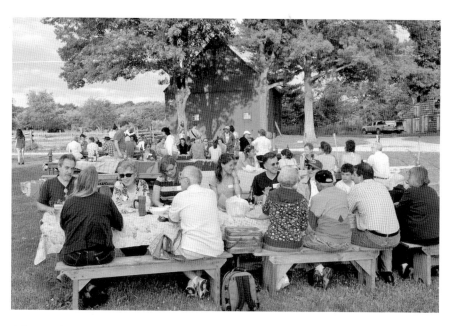

A Restoration Farm potluck dinner welcomes summer 2010. *Photo courtesy Adrian Fanning.*

composting. The harvest runs from June through October for members. Produce includes arugula, Asian greens, beets, broccoli, cabbage, carrots, cucumbers, edamame, eggplant, garlic, kale, kohlrabi, leeks, lettuce, onions, peas, peppers, potatoes, pumpkins, spinach, string beans, sweet potatoes, Swiss chard, tomatoes, turnips, winter squash, yellow squash and zucchini. Members can pick-your-own strawberries, blueberries, raspberries and blackberries in a field that is just adjacent to the Powell homestead. Several years ago, the farm added pasture-raised chickens to the mix and, in 2014, raised Berkshire pork that was served at the first farm-to-table dinner featuring a full menu made from ingredients grown on the site.

Regular community events include potluck dinners, concerts by local musicians and farm education programs on beekeeping, lacto-fermentation and backyard chickens. Fanning said that one of the benefits of Restoration Farm is its accessibility in a densely populated suburban community. "As people are looking for ways to adopt these new lifestyle changes, it's great to show them that it doesn't have to be as hard as you think," she noted. "You can just come to your local farm and hang out or buy vegetables or take a walk or go to a concert. As long as that's continuing to happen, the fact that we've lost our open space doesn't have to be the end of the story."

Restoration Farm
140 Bethpage–Sweet Hollow Road
Old Bethpage, NY, 11804
restorationfarm.com

CROSSROADS FARM AT GROSSMANN'S

Crossroads Farm at Grossmann's in Malverne is a farm in transition. After more than a century, the historic site gained a new lease on life as a five-acre farm devoted to community-sponsored organic agriculture, but the return to a fully functioning farm will take time.

Farm manager Elizabeth Schaefer described Crossroads Farm in 2014 as "a grassroots effort from the ground up," and when she talks about the ground, she really does mean the soil. More than one hundred years of farming has taken its toll. "A biodynamic soil expert literally walked onto the farm and said, 'This soil is dead,'" explained Schaefer as parched, sandy

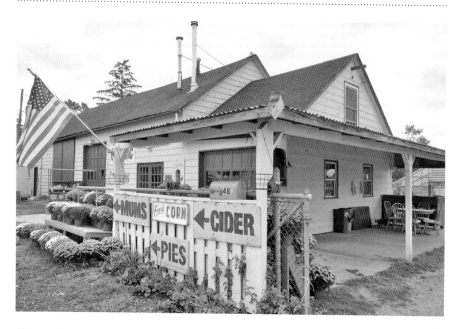

Crossroads Farm at Grossmann's in Malverne on the site of a historic family farm. *Photo by T.W. Barritt.*

soil sifted through her fingers. "My goal with the soil is to get it as healthy as possible."

Crossroads Farm at Grossmann's sits at the busy "crossroads" of Ocean and Hempstead Avenue in Malverne. The plot of land, once known simply as Grossmann's, was established as a family farm in 1895, when John Grossmann emigrated from Germany to America and began to work the land. The town of Malverne sits on a larger plot of farms once known as Norwood. By the start of the twentieth century, farms had been subdivided to accommodate new residents relocating from New York City, and the suburban district of Malverne sprung up around Grossmann's.

Four generations of the Grossmann family farmed the land. In 2007, the farm closed, and many believed that the land would be sold to developers. Nassau County acquired the property in 2009 from the Grossmann family heirs for $6.5 million through the Environmental Bond Act. The Nassau Land Trust, a not-for-profit organization whose mission is to protect and preserve Nassau County land, manages the property. Crossroads Farm at Grossmann's opened for its first growing season in 2011.

While Crossroads Farm has harvested dozens of varieties of certified organic vegetables, herbs and flowers since opening, it has yet to produce a significant yield on its own, and it has developed a direct market outlet on the property. Its business model resembles a food cooperative. Schaefer grew up on a farm and started her work career managing food cooperatives in Albany and Troy, New York. A sunny yellow building, once the Grossmann family barn, serves as the farm stand and is the face of the farm to the community.

The stand sells produce grown onsite, but it also sources vegetables and products from throughout Long Island and New York State. Through the Community Sponsored Agriculture program, farm supporters can purchase coupons redeemable for produce, baked goods and flowering plants offered at the farm stand. Volunteers who work a set number of hours a month also get a discount at the farm stand.

While Crossroads Farm at Grossmann's works to become a fully functioning farm, the small plot of land is buzzing with activity. "This farm is so unique because we're doing store and farm and education," explained Schaefer.

Strolling the property behind the farm stand, one encounters a greenhouse, rabbits, ducks, chickens, goats and herb gardens; there are plans for a petting zoo and an organic composting project. School groups and scouting programs are active on the property. There's even evidence of the farm's family legacy. A tractor dubbed "Big Blue," once owned by the Grossmann family, is still used on the site.

The farm enjoys an abundance of community goodwill, perhaps because of its history in the neighborhood. The grass-roots support that Schaefer referenced includes an active advisory board and an enthusiastic group of more than one hundred volunteers that takes on tasks at the farm stand, field work, maintenance and repairs, database entry, event planning and fundraising.

Schaefer is optimistic that Crossroads Farm at Grossmann's will continue to thrive and increase in renown. "I dream of dark earth, no weeds and really healthy vegetables," she said. "Everything here is definitely a work in progress."

Crossroads Farm at Grossmann's
480 Hempstead Avenue
Malverne, NY, 11565
516-881-7900
xroadsfarmliny.com

Bayard Cutting Arboretum CSA

While much of Long Island's former farmland has been lost to residential development, the Bayard Cutting Arboretum is an unusual example of bucking the trend. On the banks of the Connetquot River in Suffolk, an exclusive country estate—now a state park—has become a source for locally grown produce, education and community involvement.

Farm manager Jennifer Campbell was a member of the Bayard Cutting Arboretum Board of Trustees. When she walked the picturesque, manicured lawns of the estate with the executive director, she saw untapped potential. "I said, 'Wouldn't it be great to grow vegetables here?'" recalled Campbell. "This is the perfect setting for a CSA."

William Bayard Cutting was a captain of industry who lived from 1850 to 1912. His estate in Great River was called Westbrook and was planned by Frederick Law Olmsted's landscape architectural firm. Cutting was an avid gardener and nature lover, and the estate contains a varied assortment of trees, shrubs and wildflowers. The family also kept a herd of Jersey milking cows in a barn on the estate. Following his death, Cutting's family donated a portion of the estate to the Long Island State Park system for the enjoyment of the public and to inspire appreciation for the importance of informal planting.

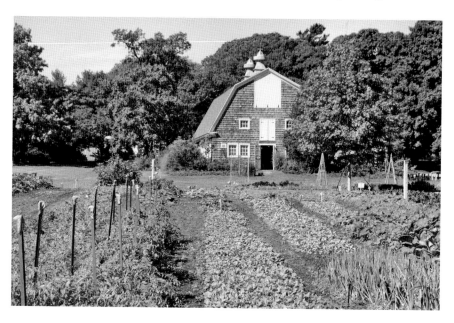

The Bayard Cutting Arboretum CSA on the grounds of a landmark estate and dairy. *Photo by T.W. Barritt.*

The arboretum's director, Nelson Sterner, supported the idea of a CSA, and an organic farm was established on the grounds in 2012. It is the state park system's only Community Sponsored Agriculture program. Eventually, Campbell took over as farm manager. She said that a CSA is a perfect complement to the mission of the arboretum, and she works hard to ensure that the aesthetic of the farm is consistent with that of the estate. "We always stop what we're doing and educate," said Campbell. "When people come here, I want them to be able to walk up and down the rows, and I want the plants to be labeled." But, she added, that meticulous care is also beneficial for the overall vegetable yield.

Campbell—who'd managed a small CSA, worked at a nursery and has a master gardener certificate—said that more than one hundred families take a share in the farm. The historic dairy barn is used for vegetable pickups, and a separate calving barn houses a flock of chickens. Weekly events encourage members to socialize and tend to the farm. Campbell noted that the program is a productive use of state property and yields additional benefits for members beyond nutrition, including a sense of ownership. "I feel strongly about the community aspect of CSA," she said. "I know everybody; I want them to participate and get their hands in the soil."

Bayard Cutting Arboretum CSA
440 Montauk Highway
Great River, NY, 11739
631-256-5048
bayardcuttingarboretum.com/farm

The Long Island Fair

For two weekends each autumn, thousands of Long Islanders travel back to a simpler era via the Long Island Fair, held annually at Old Bethpage Village Restoration. In the heart of twenty-first-century suburbia, neighbors turn out to engage in bucolic, homespun pursuits such as quilting, needlework, gardening and baking competitions and might indulge in a crisp local apple or a cider doughnut for a snack.

The Long Island Fair is one of the authentic descendants of Long Island's agrarian roots and has had many incarnations. Initially, it was a festival sponsored by the Agricultural Society of Queens in 1842. At that time, the fair was organized and held on open fields and farms owned by the society's

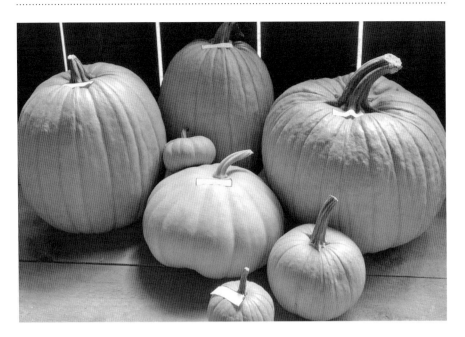

Award-winning squash at the Long Island Fair, held annually at Old Bethpage Village. *Photo by T.W. Barritt.*

members. In 1866, a permanent fairground was established on Old Country Road and Washington Avenue in Mineola, which is the site of the Nassau County Courthouse today. An elaborate exhibition hall was erected at the center of the fairgrounds and was the location for the Queens County Fair until 1899 (the year that Nassau County was established and the fair was renamed the Mineola Fair).

According to Old Bethpage Village historian Gary R. Hammond in his monograph "The Mineola Fair: Mirror of a County's Growth," the fair was a barometer of the area's economic prosperity. It was an important community function that attracted local luminaries. Then New York State governor Theodore Roosevelt delivered a speech at the 1899 fair and dined on the local victuals offered at the event.

For fifty years, the fair continued at the Old Country Road site, but it was eventually relocated to Roosevelt Raceway. In 1970, a permanent home for the fair was established at Old Bethpage Village Restoration. A public effort raised funds to construct a facsimile of the original Mineola fairground, and a replica of the exhibition hall was completed in 1995.

The modern fair has not strayed from its origins and boasts a full schedule of events, exhibits and blue ribbon competitions celebrating cooking, baking,

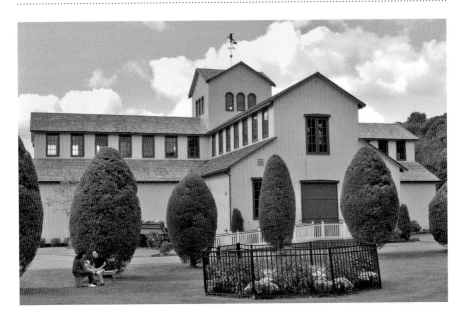

The reconstructed exhibition hall at the Long Island Fair, Old Bethpage Village. *Photo by T.W. Barritt.*

agriculture and animal husbandry. A hefty "premium book" distributed in advance of the festivities solicits entries in contests for jams and jellies, pickled vegetables, yeast breads and cakes, floral arrangements and needlework. Poultry, rabbits, guinea pigs and draft horses compete for best in show, and fruits and vegetables are judged on size, quality and appearance. There's even a modern "Think Green" competition that awards prizes for recycling and repurposing items in creative and functional ways, as well as lively competitions throughout the fairgrounds devoted to scarecrow making and crosscut sawing. As in days of yore, outdoor food merchants selling fresh doughnuts and grilled corn keep visitors well nourished.

The Long Island Fair
PO Box 151
Sea Cliff, NY, 11579
516-874-0502
lifair.org

Old Bethpage Village Restoration
1303 Round Swamp Road
Old Bethpage, NY, 11804

Long Island Growers Market

It took the stewards of one of the oldest family farms on Long Island to reimagine how Long Islanders would shop for local produce. In the process, they revitalized their three-hundred-year-old farm and created a new distribution channel for farmers and aspiring food artisans.

While open-air food markets have existed in Europe for centuries, Long Island's first community farmers' market wasn't established until 1991. It would be romantic to think that the Islip Farmers' Market emerged purely out of the public's desire for locally grown food, but it was really an economic necessity for the farmers involved. Ethel and Fred Terry of Fred Terry Farms in Orient have been the orchestrators of the growth in farmers' markets on Long Island over the past two decades.

"We were a huge wholesaler for many years, and every year we wound up more and more in debt," said Ethel Terry. Fees to the produce house, brokers and truckers left the Terrys with minimal profit. In addition, an influx of out-of-state produce was forcing prices down even more. The Terrys decided to take control of their own distribution and sell directly to the public. "We realized there was a lot more money to be made and a lot more profit to be made by going strictly retail," added Ethel.

They began making the transition slowly, loading a small pickup truck with produce and making the long trip from Orient at the eastern end of Long Island to sell at the greenmarkets in New York City. It was a courageous and game-changing move for a historic family farm.

Fred Terry Farms is a 120-acre farm that sits on the North Fork, within a half mile of the Orient Point Ferry that connects to New London, Connecticut. The Terry family was originally from England and acquired the land in 1732, when Jonathan Terry purchased the property from Joshua Curtis. Jonathan was the great-grandson of Thomas Terry, one of the early settlers of Southold. In total, seven generations have farmed the land, which is still maintained by Fred and Ethel Terry today.

Ethel Terry suggested that modern economic pressures have put the farm at risk. "Farmers are like dinosaurs," she said. "We're in extinction." Yet the family found a way to evolve. Eventually, they expanded to additional greenmarkets in New York City. The transformation required a crop change. The Terrys had grown potatoes and cabbage to service the wholesale market, but shoppers at farmers' markets were seeking variety. "In order to survive at the farmers' market, you have to have something different than the supermarket," said Ethel. "We grow five different

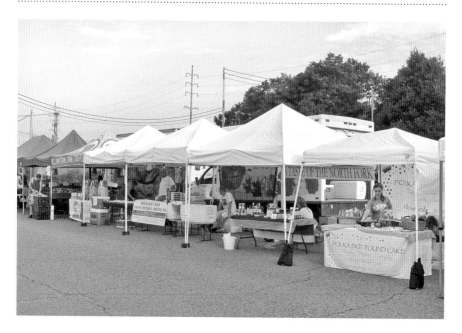

The Long Island Growers Market operates farmers' markets throughout Nassau and Suffolk. *Photo by T.W. Barritt.*

kinds of beets, we grow four different kinds of carrots and we grow seven different kinds of peppers."

One day—at a market at the World Trade Center—the Terrys were approached by a Long Island resident who asked the couple if they would like to help establish a recurring farmers' market in the town of Islip. Working in cooperation with community leaders, the Islip Farmers' Market was established in 1991. Today, it operates weekly at the Islip Town Hall parking lot from May through November. Other municipalities took note, and Ethel Terry founded the Long Island Growers Market to manage the growing demand and feature merchants from all over Long Island. Since 1991, the organization has run up to seventeen farmers' markets in a season and has established a model for transparency between vendors and customers. "We only allow vendors to sell what they make, bake, grow or catch," said Ethel. "We do not allow brokers in our market." Food offerings include fruits and vegetables, wine, goat cheese, seafood, honey, olive oils, jams and jellies, soup stocks, spreads and even homemade doggy treats.

The Long Island Growers Market recognizes that more consumers are seeking verification of the source of their food. There is a rigorous vendor

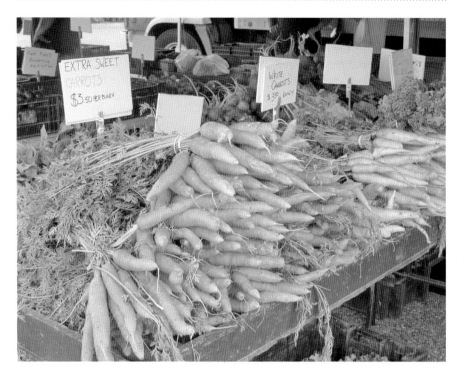

Fresh produce at the Long Island Growers Market in Seaford. *Photo by T.W. Barritt.*

approval process, which includes site inspections. "Before I put a farmer in, I personally visit, because I am a farmer," said Ethel. "You can't pull the wool over my eyes."

She said that customers are more educated than ever before. "They come and they ask questions. They look you in the eye, and they want to know where their food is coming from."

During the 2014 growing season, the Long Island Growers Market managed farmers' markets in Huntington Village, Islip, Patchogue, Port Jefferson, Riverhead, Garden City, Locust Valley, Rockville Centre, Roslyn and Seaford. So many communities have shown an interest in establishing markets that the Long Island Growers Market has a waiting list. "We're so well established and so well respected that they come to us," said Ethel.

For the Terrys, the transformation of their business model has not altered the physical demands of running a farming operation. "We're on the road about quarter of four in the morning heading out to our markets, and then we get home and unload and get ready for the next day," noted Ethel. In between, they are working the farm.

"My husband and I do everything," she said. "We do all the planting, which starts at the greenhouse, and then we transplant out to the fields." It remains a family effort, and while Fred is the last of the Terry line, his stepson will take over the farm should the couple decide to retire. For now, they are embracing the new chapter they've written in the ongoing history of Fred Terry Farms. "You get such pride in telling people you really live off the land," said Ethel.

Long Island Growers Market
35870 Main Road
Orient, NY, 11957
631-323-3653
longislandgrowersmarket.com

KERBER'S FARM

Nick Voulgaris III saw something special in the dilapidated farm stand on West Pulaski Road in Huntington that had sat abandoned for years. The entrepreneur, author and Huntington native had fond memories of visits to Kerber's Farm growing up in the 1970s and 1980s. In fact, the farm (originally owned by the Peter Kerber family, who built a local reputation selling fresh chicken, pies, produce and ice cream) had been a Huntington fixture since 1941. "I'm very nostalgic," said Voulgaris. "I appreciate classic things, and I'm also a traditionalist."

When the former poultry farm property was targeted for development as condominiums, Voulgaris began to imagine the possibilities of restoring Kerber's to its heyday. "I thought it was crazy that this place was abandoned," he said. "I knew if I could reopen what it was, and preserve its name and its legacy, it would be successful."

Voulgaris—who has a background in hospitality and food service—purchased the property in early 2013 and began a painstaking restoration, doing much of the work himself. "It was horrendous," he explained, but he kept focused on the potential, including the fact that his research showed that an estimated fourteen thousand cars drove past the property daily.

The site offered a unique business opportunity for Voulgaris, as it is zoned for agriculture and commercial use. Kerber's Farm includes a storefront,

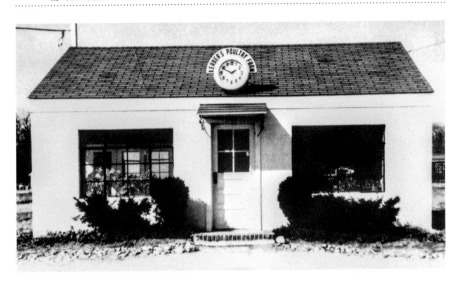

Kerber's Poultry Farm, circa 1950. *Photo courtesy Kerber's Farm.*

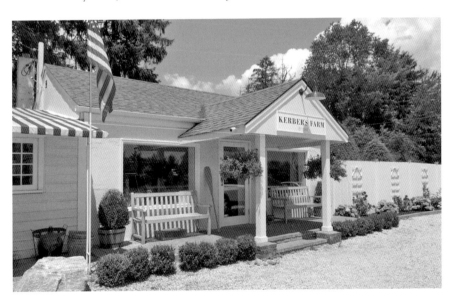

The newly restored Kerber's Farm in Huntington. *Photo by T.W. Barritt.*

two houses, six barns and a 150-foot-long chicken coop. Some of the barns are salvaged World War II army barracks that were bought as surplus and trucked in.

Voulgaris relaunched Kerber's Farm on Labor Day weekend of 2013. In a nod to Kerber's heritage, the newly designed logo features an iconic

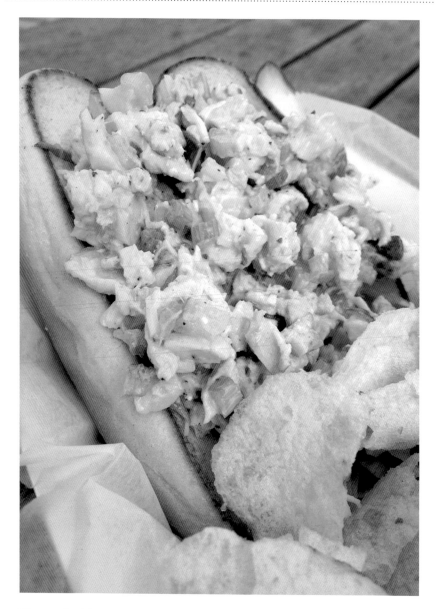

The popular lobster roll served at Kerber's Farm. *Photo by T.W. Barritt.*

graphic of a heritage chicken. The farm stand combines a homespun aesthetic with a touch of East End cachet. The buildings are whitewashed and festooned with smart, green-striped awnings. Inside there are high ceilings with exposed beams, and Sinatra croons from the stereo speakers.

"Found" items—such as antique birdcages, nautical items and wooden bread bowls—are offered for sale in the shop.

The farm store sells a variety of homemade jam, preserves, pies and baked goods, including a popular cheddar buttermilk biscuit for breakfast. Honey is harvested and sold from hives on the site. All of the baked goods are prepared from scratch. During the summer months, Kerber's sells organic produce grown on the property. Roasted corn, long a staple at Kerber's, is served along with fresh lobster rolls, which evoke summer on Long Island to Voulgaris, a yachting enthusiast. A small flock of hens produces organic eggs, and Voulgaris hopes to restore the original chicken coop on the site over time. During the autumn and winter months, Kerber's sells pumpkins, apples, mulled apple cider and homemade cider donuts. A holiday shop features vintage Christmas ornaments.

Voulgaris has been touched by the overwhelming response from the community. "I get letters from strangers and all sorts of notes in the mail thanking me for preserving this, for investing in the community and for saving a landmark."

Voulgaris is proud that he is "creating a place that embodies certain values from the past." He sees Kerber's legacy of nostalgia, hospitality and quality influencing a new generation of Long Islanders. "Hopefully, this will be known as one of the best places on Long Island to buy pies and really wholesome, natural foods," he said, "and a place that has a certain style and flair."

Kerber's Farm
309 West Pulaski Road
Huntington, NY, 11743
631-423-4400
kerbersfarm.com

Orkestai Farm

Located on the grounds of Planting Fields Arboretum State Historic Park in Oyster Bay, Orkestai Farm is a one-acre holistic farm devoted to "expressive agriculture." It provides a safe, creative community and a sensory experience for adolescents and adults with autism and other developmental disabilities. "Orkestai" is derived from an ancient Greek word, *orkheisthai*, which refers to the idea of collaborative movement.

Orkestai Farm looks to agriculture to provide therapeutic benefits beyond nutrition and sustenance. The farm accepts between fifteen and twenty student farmers, who sign up to participate in two-hour blocks of individualized farm education twice a week during the growing season. Through engagement in the daily activities and rhythms of farming, student farmers—who often lack verbal skills and encounter challenges moving through daily life—learn to move, collaborate and accomplish agricultural tasks and share in a productive community effort. Co–Executive Director Erin Staub said that workshops are small by design. "We want to keep a peaceful environment for everyone to work and to learn."

Co–Executive Director Alethea Vasilas added that the idea of a farm for "differently abled individuals" first took shape when she mentored a young woman with autism. They spent a day working at Vasilas's organic family farm in Orient, and she noted the positive impact the recurring movements of farm activity had on the woman.

"That day, she must have planted six hundred tomato plants with me," said Vasilas. "Farming seemed to support her natural rhythms. It's both calming work and predictable and supportive in that way."

By the end of that day, the woman proclaimed that she wanted to become a farmer. The woman's mother—who was active in the autism community—founded SustainAbility Farm at Planting Fields in 2011 as a farming environment to support people with autism and other disabilities. Vasilas served as farm and project manager for the 2013 growing season. When the family relocated upstate to establish a farmstead residence, Vasilas joined with Erin Staub as co–executive directors to continue and build the program as Orkestai Farm.

The Planting Fields Arboretum preserves a self-contained community of an earlier era. Originally composed of six farming properties once referred to as Upper Planting Fields Farm, it is the site of the sixty-five-room Coe Hall estate—one of Long Island's famed Gold Coast mansions—completed in 1921 and built to resemble an Elizabethan manor. The owner, William Robertson Coe, was fascinated by horticulture, and the mansion is surrounded by greenhouses and meticulously tended gardens. The transformation of Planting Fields to a State Historic Park and the emergence of Orkestai Farm are more evidence of efforts to enrich the community through innovative use of Long Island's historic land and open spaces.

Vasilas said that the farm and the work environment provide a sensory experience for the student farmers and that each farmer gleans different benefits depending on their challenges in daily life. For some, the program offers the ability to learn pre-vocational skills. Others benefit from the social interaction. Often it is simply the movement of planting and harvesting that enhances their work. The farmers are encouraged to take home the food they grow and experience vegetables they might never have tried.

"There is a therapeutic aspect to the environment and the work we do together," said Vasilas. She noted that in other cultures, music, dance and movement are integrated into agricultural rituals and that, as a trained dancer, this also informs her work.

The sense of community experienced in the field can have a ripple effect beyond Orkestai Farm. "When you grow food and create food, you are really helping to create people's bodies," said Vasilas. "The work that you have done in the field becomes very real on a cellular level."

About twenty to twenty-five community members participate in a Community Sponsored Agriculture program. Staub said that the CSA members are extremely supportive. "They stay, they have lunch with us and they've gotten to know our farmers," she explained. "We try to hold a lot of community events so they all get to work together."

"We're trying to become more deliberate and more observing," said Vasilas. "I hope that somehow we can influence Long Island to just take a breath and slow down and cultivate relationships with everyone that makes up our community. We have a lot to learn from our farmers, for sure."

Orkestai Farm
1395 Planting Fields Road
Oyster Bay, NY, 11771
516-817-6420
orkestaifarm.org

Chapter 2
Agricultural Innovators

What will the farm of the future look like? As Long Island grapples with diminishing open space and a growing demand for culinary innovation, noteworthy models are emerging that suggest potential answers. Koppert Cress and Thera Farms could both easily be put in the category of "artisan greens," but each has a very different mission. More than EPCOT-style marvels, each is a viable business enterprise. Much like the immigrant farms of the past that sprang up to provide new produce options to nearby city dwellers, these agricultural innovators are putting down literal roots, employing science and technology and upending traditional culinary practices to change the way Long Islanders eat.

Koppert Cress

Nicholas Mazard stands in a sprawling glass complex just off Route 48 in Cutchogue, surrounded by an expanse of micro-greens the size of several football fields. It is an overcast winter day, but the afternoon light is amplified by the panels on the thirty-thousand-square-foot glass house, casting a burnished aura over the field of emerald and red micro-greens. The tender baby greens are about two inches tall, with perfectly shaped leaves. While the greens are diminutive in size, they contain tremendous flavor. Mazard calls the glass house a "Willy Wonka factory."

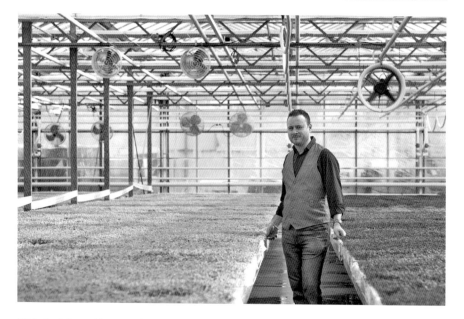

Nicholas Mazard is general manager of Koppert Cress, which grows micro-greens in Cutchogue. *Photo by Jacob Skoglund.*

The passionate Mazard—a native of France—is general manager of Koppert Cress USA, the stateside headquarters for a micro-green company that got its start in the Netherlands. The owners launched their U.S. operation in Cutchogue, Long Island, in 2006. With three hundred days of sunshine annually, Cutchogue is the ideal location to cultivate micro-greens and a perfect location from which to market to top chefs based in Manhattan and Long Island's East End.

The vision of an endless carpet of micro-greens can only be described as otherworldly. However one chooses to describe the experience, there is one word that is strictly prohibited. Don't *ever* call them "sprouts."

Mazard pinches a few succulent green leaves and passes them to a visitor to taste. He waits expectantly for a reaction. A familiar, buttery flavor fills the visitor's mouth. It tastes like a tangy slice of Brie cheese, quite unexpected from a snip of fresh greens.

The heady rush of flavor continues. Delicate blush pink leaves pop with the flavor of apple blossoms. Snips of greens evoke bursts of bright citrus, earthy mushrooms, pungent pepper, hot wasabi, Dijon mustard and even salty oysters. It's all grown naturally, and Koppert Cress is leading the gastronomic trend to dress restaurant plates with lush, flavorful greens.

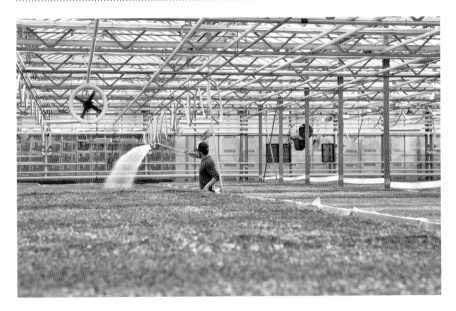

Koppert Cress harvests micro-greens for chefs to use in a wide range of dishes. *Photo by Jacob Skoglund.*

A "cress" is a small plant with spicy leaves, often used in salads. Koppert Cress goes far beyond the typical salad ingredients and draws on international flavor profiles, foraging techniques, aromatherapy and herbology, turning the concept of "heirloom varieties" on its head. Mazard calls the micro-greens "a living condiment." Koppert Cress maintains a carefully curated flavor collection of nearly seventy-five varieties of micro-greens from across the globe, and the company gives careful attention to the history and ethnicity of each plant. "I find it fascinating that a plant was used by people for thousands of years," said Mazard.

Micro-greens are sourced from far-flung locations such as India, the Middle East, Japan, the Mediterranean and the Himalayas. Koppert Cress offers three varieties to chefs: living micro-greens, cut micro-greens and specialty micro-greens. The micro-greens are germinated in clean, natural fiber and are provided with tasting notes and culinary recommendations. For example, Micro Basil Lemon is suggested for use with fish, crustaceans and scallops, while Micro Tangerine complements seafood dishes, desserts and vodka cocktails.

The company has opened a second location in Riverhead and plans to develop a visitors' center there. The glass growing houses are climate controlled. Large flats of micro-greens, stacked in two levels, rotate throughout the glass house on a computerized conveyor system to optimize exposure to the sun. It is a year-round growing season, and micro-greens are shipped to chefs throughout the United States. A crop is harvested every eighteen days, but the growers must sow almost every day because customers need the product available on a daily basis. "We're the most intense farmers in the world," said Managing Director Eddy Creces.

Mazard is on a mission to inspire chefs. "We give chefs new opportunities," he said. "We bring them a wider palette of color for whatever they're painting, but the masterpiece is still theirs." Yet he asserted emphatically that micro-greens are much more than an aesthetically pleasing decoration. "What you are going to put on your plate will bring something to your plate—not just visually but with underlying flavor, intensity of flavor and balance of flavor."

Koppert Cress USA
23423 Middle Road/Route 48
Cutchogue, NY, 11935
631-743-8500
usa.koppertcress.com

Thera Farms

A malicious spring snowstorm is pounding the walls of the greenhouse at the three-acre Thera Farms in Ronkonkoma. Inside, owner Teddy Bolkas—dressed in a T-shirt, shorts and a straw hat—radiates warmth and happiness. It's almost as if his positive energy is feeding the multiple rows of pristine, hydroponic lettuce that fill the twenty-six- by one-hundred-foot interior.

Harvesting fresh lettuce in late March on the East Coast is improbable at best, but several years ago, Bolkas built a do-it-yourself hydroponic system at Thera Farm. He harvests weekly, yielding ten thousand heads of lettuce per year. His customers are thrilled, particularly in winter months, when locally grown lettuce is hard to come by. The alternating rows of perfectly formed Boston lettuce and Red Boston resemble lush bridal bouquets.

"It's a lot of lettuce for a little space," said Bolkas. "I can produce as much in this greenhouse as I would in over two acres of land, and I can do it with 90 percent less water, less nutrients and no bug sprays because I control the atmosphere."

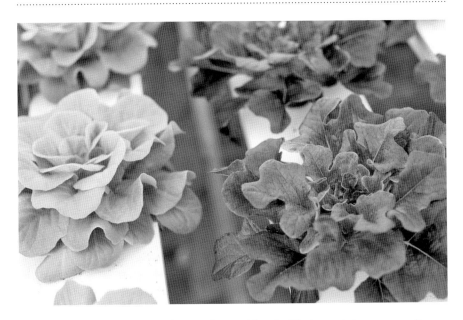

Thera Farms in Ronkonkoma raises ten thousand heads of hydroponic lettuce annually. *Photo by Jacob Skoglund.*

The practice of hydroponics uses a nutrient-enriched, pH-balanced water solution to grow plants without soil. A reservoir contains the blend of water and nutrients, which is fed through narrow lines to plastic troughs containing the plants. The water circulates twenty-four hours per day, and an electronic system monitors the temperature, pH and nutrient levels. Seedlings are started in clean fiber and then transferred to the growing trough, where their roots drink in the water pumped through the trough.

Thera Farms is surrounded by suburban split-level homes. Concealed behind a house, the farm is easy to miss, but the "secret garden" hidden within the greenhouse contains a surprising bounty. Bolkas grows both hydroponic lettuce and arugula and has been experimenting with broccoli rabe. He said that leafy greens are particularly well suited to hydroponics.

Bolkas was seven years old, and didn't speak a word of English, when his family emigrated from Greece in 1982. The family kept seventeen goats on the Ronkonkoma property. He explained that at the time, nobody wanted goat cheese, so eventually the family transitioned to raising tomatoes. Bolkas now manages the small organic operation. In addition to hydroponic lettuce, he offers heirloom tomatoes (cultivated outdoors), fresh pastel-colored eggs from his brood of laying hens, figs and pasture-raised beef from a farm he established in upstate New York. He markets his product through a farm

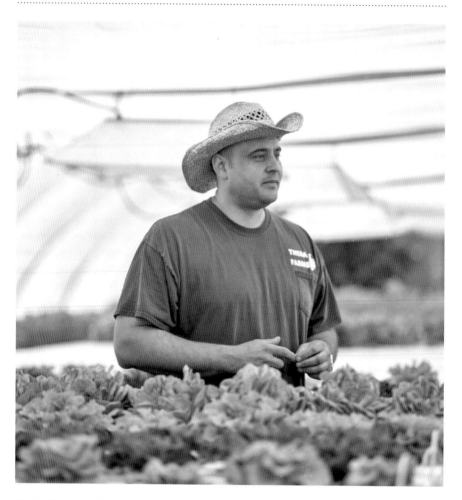

Teddy Bolkas of Thera Farms pioneered hydroponic lettuce on Long Island. *Photo by Jacob Skoglund.*

stand on the property, a website that offers home delivery and through participation in seasonal farmers' markets.

Bolkas has gained some notoriety for being one of the first growers in the region to embrace hydroponics. Others are beginning to follow suit. He first considered hydroponic farming as a practical way to increase production and add value to his business.

"We're small, and we're popular," said Bolkas. "So per square foot, I need to grow a lot of stuff." He purchased a complete hydroponic kit that took him about a week to set up, including the reservoir, food-grade plastic troughs and digital meters that monitor the growing environment.

He expanded the system as demand grew and can produce a full head of lettuce two weeks faster than it would typically take to mature in an outdoor growing environment. He retains the long root system and wraps the roots in a damp napkin, which he calls "a diaper." That helps the lettuce keep in the refrigerator for over a week. His customers keep coming back for more and tell him that the blemish-free, flavorful "living lettuce" is "hands down the best they've ever had."

Bolkas seems to relish his role as a neighborhood farmer. "Once you start doing it, you just get addicted, and you can't stop," he said. "People are healthy because of me! What's cooler than that? It's amazing!"

He indicated that the move to hydroponics was a crucial part of his survival and success as an agricultural entrepreneur and has implications for agriculture on Long Island, where concern for the environment is growing and land is becoming scarce. "You've got to try new things," he said. "If you don't change, you're going to die."

He welcomes visitors to the farm, where a lively playlist of oldies tunes fills the greenhouse. It's all part of the upbeat vibe at Thera Farms. "Plants have feelings," said Bolkas. "The better mood that you're in, the happier they are and the better they grow."

One taste and you'll be convinced that this is happy lettuce.

Thera Farms
2256 Motor Parkway
Ronkonkoma, NY, 11779
631-478-5229
TheraFarms.com

Chapter 3
Mollusks, Fins and Gills

The Native American tribes who once inhabited Long Island were "eating local" centuries before the idea ever became a slogan of the Slow Food movement. Native tribes built camps at inlets along the shore—where freshwater streams met saltwater bays—to harvest the seemingly endless bounty of the sea. They fished with bows and arrows and primitive hooks, gathering bluefish, bass and herring. Archaeological evidence shows that shellfish were a significant component of their diet. The shallow bay waters that surround Long Island yielded a plentiful supply. Native Americans steamed shellfish in coal pits or atop hot stones and feasted on oysters, scallops, crabs, soft-shell clams, hard-shell clams and lobsters. The Shinnecock tribe was said to have placed tree branches in the bay waters to cultivate oysters. The young oysters would attach themselves to the branches early in their development, and the branches would be placed in protected salt ponds along the South Shore until the oysters reached maturity.

European settlers clearly were captivated by Long Island's rich maritime resources and would adopt the name of its most bountiful bivalve. In 1639, voyager David deVries anchored in the waters north of Long Island. He noted in his diary the fine quality of the oysters he'd discovered in the surrounding waters and that the Dutch settlers referred to the area as Oyster Bay.

In 1661, six English families settled in the area at Long Island's easternmost point, which is known today as the towns of Orient and East Marion. They named their new home Oysterponds for the copious supply

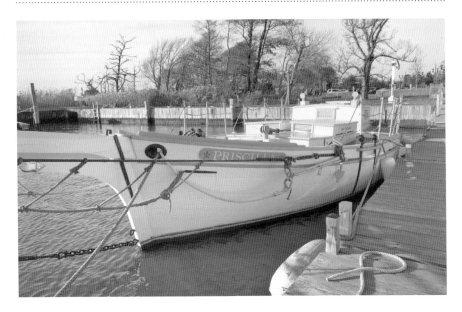

The oyster sloop *Priscilla*, first launched in 1888, West Sayville. *Photo by T.W. Barritt.*

of shellfish they found. They collected these for their own consumption and also sold them to neighboring residents.

As more and more settlers populated Long Island, they devised new and ingenious ways to gather the prized oysters. In the waters off the south shore of Seaford, baymen found it challenging to maneuver their boats due to the irregular land hidden just below the shallow ocean water. In the mid-1800s, they built a flat-bottomed boat, which was dubbed the *Seaford Skiff*. The streamlined boat allowed them to move among the shallow waters without rowing.

At one point in the nineteenth century, there were nearly five hundred oyster dredging sloops that worked the South Shore of Long Island. The *Priscilla* is the oldest preserved oyster sloop of that era and can be seen at the Long Island Maritime Museum in West Sayville. Originally built in 1888 in Patchogue and restored in 2002 and 2003, the sloop was designated as a National Historic Landmark in 2006. Powered by sail, the *Priscilla* measures sixty feet in length and is typical of the type of craft once used to haul dredges—or large scoops—across shellfish beds collecting oysters.

Fishing also flourished. Like the Native Americans, communities clustered close to the source of food and economic opportunity along waterways. Fishing communities sprang up in Brookhaven, Patchogue, West Sayville and Freeport. Maritime resources became interdependent with agriculture.

A type of fish called menhaden—which was not suitable for food—was caught in large quantities and used for fertilizer in farming. A vibrant whaling industry developed, and President George Washington designated the whaling center of Sag Harbor along with New York City as the first two ports of entry in the nation. Baymen caught fluke, flounder, eel and striped bass. The Doxsee Clam Company was established in 1865 in Islip, but by 1900, the company had closed, as the supply of clams was depleted in the Great South Bay.

Legend claims that Joseph Avery of Blue Point planted oyster seed that he acquired from Maryland's Chesapeake Bay in the waters near Blue Point in 1815. Supposedly, he christened the oysters he harvested as Blue Point Oysters, named for the bluish haze that often settled over his hometown. As early evidence of the power of branding, the name stuck, and Blue Point Oysters gained worldwide recognition. It is one of many examples of a foodstuff transplanted and adopted by Long Island. The name was often appropriated, and in 1908, New York State passed legislation prohibiting the use of the name Blue Point Oyster by any oysters not cultivated in the Great South Bay. However, the law proved difficult to enforce.

By the early 1900s, Long Island had become a world center for oyster production. Oyster shanties were a common sight along the South Shore.

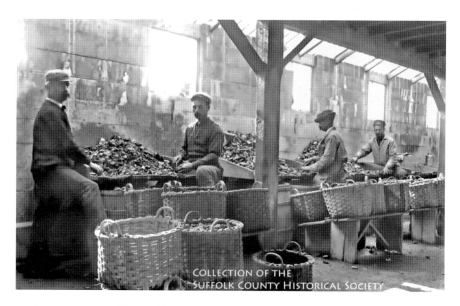

Sorting oysters, circa 1900, by Hal B. Fullerton. *From the Harry T. Tuthill Fullerton Collection of the Suffolk County Historical Society. Copyright © Suffolk County Historical Society. All rights reserved.*

The William Rudolph Oyster House is preserved today at the Long Island Maritime Museum and is a fine example of the type of rustic structure where baymen shucked and sorted oysters. Inevitably, it was Dutch oysterman Jacob Ockers who solidified the Blue Point Oyster's place in culinary history. In 1912, Ockers founded the Bluepoints Oyster Company on Atlantic Avenue in West Sayville. The company would become the largest producer of oysters in the world. Huge numbers of Dutch immigrants—who had learned shellfish harvesting in their homeland—worked the bay and the oyster houses. The rise of the Long Island Railroad provided new opportunities to ship oysters to restaurants in New York and markets beyond.

Several factors contributed to the decline of the Long Island oyster industry. Devastating storms altered the composition of natural oyster beds, and pollution, algae, Brown Tide and changing consumer preferences all took their toll. Yet in the past decade there have been efforts to revive oyster production. A number of producers have had great success seeding and cultivating oysters in Long Island bay waters. Blue Island Oyster Company in West Sayville is well established, and smaller operators are making names for themselves in local aquaculture. The Aeros Cultivated Oyster Company sells Peconic Pearls and Mystic Oysters, farmed at a hatchery near Southold that was once owned by the Shelter Island Oyster Company but which closed in the 1950s. In 2011, the Town of Islip initiated a novel program encouraging local entrepreneurs to lease acreage for shellfish aquaculture in the Great South Bay. Aspiring baymen were and are encouraged to cultivate American oyster, hard clam, bay scallop, blue mussel, soft-shell clam and razor clam.

The noble oyster is never far from our collective consciousness or our collective appetites. Each year in October, the Oyster Festival is held in Oyster Bay, and it hosts more than 200,000 visitors from up and down the East Coast. It is the largest outdoor festival on Long Island, featuring salty, succulent oysters prepared a variety of ways, as well as oyster eating and oyster shucking contests.

On the South Fork of Long Island, history has come full circle at the Shinnecock Indian Nation, where more than seven hundred members of the tribe reside near Southampton. Beginning in 1973, the tribe established the Shinnecock Oyster Project, and today the privately held Shinnecock Oyster Farm cultivates a trademarked brand of oyster known as Tomahawk.

Blue Island Oyster Company

Chris Quartuccio, the lanky chief executive officer of Blue Island Oyster Company in West Sayville, may well be the modern-day incarnation of Joseph Avery, the legendary Long Island oysterman. Avery, a resident of Blue Point whose home still stands on Middle Road, marketed his locally raised Blue Point Oysters shrewdly, putting a uniquely Long Island product on tables around the world and inspiring a global industry. Quartuccio grew up in Sayville in the 1970s, when thousands of people made their living harvesting clams in the Great South Bay. It's the same district from which the Long Island oyster industry emerged, and locals claim that the streets are paved with oyster shells.

"It was a very easy business to get into," said Quartuccio. "All you had to do was walk along the shoreline and catch the clams with your feet."

At the age of twelve, Quartuccio was already scoping out the potential business opportunity. "There were probably about twelve clam bars from Bayport to West Sayville," he explained. "All you had to do was bring your clams there, and they would hand you cash." Quartuccio earned money clamming through middle school, high school and college.

After college, he worked in the fashion industry in New York City and waited tables at night to earn extra cash. "I had access to the price list from the seafood company in the restaurant, and I could see these restaurants were paying thirty cents for clams," he recalled. "I really didn't like working in the fashion industry and figured if I could dig clams on Long Island and sell them for thirty cents I could make a pretty good living."

He began approaching high-end restaurants in Manhattan to solicit business. He made his first sale in 1995 to the posh Lenox Room on Manhattan's Upper East Side, co-owned by Chef Charlie Palmer. The invoice for that sale is now framed and hangs on the wall in his office at the Blue Island Oyster Company.

"I would drive out here, and I would harvest clams and bring them back to the city," said Quartuccio. About six months later, some acquaintances asked him if he could sell a load of wild oysters they'd harvested in the bay. "I'd never seen a live oyster," said Quartuccio. "I grabbed some and took them to the Lenox Room, and that's when I realized you could make a lot more money on the oysters."

It was long before the farm-to-table movement, and oysters did not enjoy the popularity that they do today. Quartuccio—who was diver certified—discovered quickly that the freshness of oysters delivered straight from the

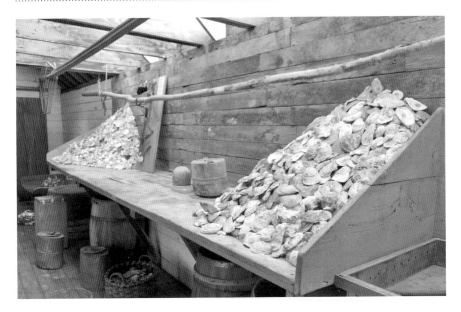

Interior of the historic William Rudolph Oyster House, West Sayville. *Photo by T.W. Barritt.*

ocean held great appeal for New York restaurateurs. "It was an easy sell," he explained. "I would go in there, sunburned and salt crusted on me, and you could smell me, and I'm delivering these things around 3:00 p.m. and they were harvested that day—boom—right into the restaurant."

Today, oyster bars are featured in restaurants all over the country. Quartuccio's business, Blue Island Oyster Company, sits at the end of a street in West Sayville lined by homes once occupied by the Dutch immigrants who worked the oyster beds of the Great South Bay in the 1800s. Quartuccio founded the company in 1995. Blue Island Oyster Company connects the past to the present, marketing some 700,000 oysters annually en route.

"I really believe that we pioneered modern aquaculture in the Great South Bay," he said. "We were the first to successfully grow oysters since the hurricane of 1938. It's a genuine Blue Point Oyster that has all the flavors of the Blue Point of years ago."

Oysters are spawned in a hatchery. When they reach the size of a dime, they are transferred to an underwater farm near the Fire Island Inlet in the Great South Bay or the Peconic Bay to grow to maturity. "Just like wine, oysters take on the flavor of their location," said Quartuccio. "All three bay waters taste different. The Great South Bay oysters have this vegetal, celery salt tone."

The company markets both farmed and wild oysters. Blue Island Oysters and Oak Beach Oysters are farmed in the Great South Bay. Peconic

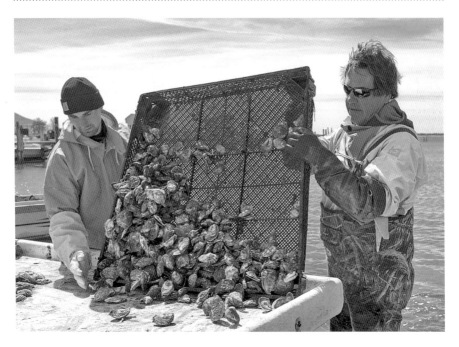

The team at West Sayville's Blue Island Oyster Company harvests oysters. *Photo by Richard Bowditch.*

Bay Oysters are farmed in Peconic Bay, and Naked Cowboy Oysters are harvested wild from Long Island Sound.

"We're the ones responsible for bringing the oyster industry back," said Quartuccio. "As a company, it's probably our greatest achievement to date."

Blue Island Oyster Company
136 Atlantic Avenue
West Sayville, NY, 11798
631-563-1330
blueislandoyster.com

Dock to Dish

Inspired by the Community Sponsored Agriculture model, Dock to Dish invites members to make an investment in Long Island's ocean resources and get to know their fisherman personally. Conceived by local fisherman and restaurateur Sean Barrett, the ambitious seafood cooperative was founded in 2012, drawing attention to sustainable fishing practices and the variety of seafood sourced from Long Island waters.

Organizers point out that more than 90 percent of seafood consumed in the United States is imported. They are out to change that, aiming to establish local hubs that can distribute the freshest seafood to individuals and restaurants. It is both an exercise in informed eating and an evolving business model that could reinvigorate the local seafood marketplace. The ocean waters that line the Hamptons and Montauk region are a haven for marinas, commercial fishermen, charter boats and fly-fishing enthusiasts. More than forty commercial fishermen and shellfish harvesters participate in the Dock to Dish program. The fishermen must be licensed, follow the fishing guidelines of the National Oceanic and Atmospheric Administration (NOAA) and adhere to a Dock to Dish code of ethics.

Dock to Dish members prepay for a weekly delivery that can run between fourteen and twenty weeks. The popular program has sold out each season since its inception. Individual and family memberships include a weekly share of fresh, locally sourced fish filets in quantities of two and four pounds. Members can pick up their weekly share at designated locations on the East End of Long Island and transport the fish in special insulated bags. All fish is certified to have left the dock no more than twenty-four hours after having been brought in. This practice ensures that members are receiving the freshest fish possible. Dock to Dish offers a rotating selection of more than twenty different fish and shellfish varieties. The selection includes premium fish and bycatch (fish that might have otherwise been discarded) indigenous to the waters of Long Island and New England, such as sea robin, black sea bass, blowfish, bluefish, haddock, swordfish, monkfish and summer flounder.

Dock to Dish also works directly with several top-line Long Island and New York City restaurants, providing weekly deliveries of one hundred pounds of local fish. Noted chefs such as Dan Barber of Blue Hill Restaurant have embraced the fresh catch as a featured item on their farm-to-table menus.

Dock to Dish services members in Montauk, Amagansett, Sag Harbor and the Hamptons. Organizers have launched a second cooperative in Key West, with others planned for the port cities of Key Largo and Miami.

Dock to Dish
6 South Elmwood Avenue
Montauk, NY, 11954
917-853-8559
docktodish.com

Freeport's Nautical Mile

The area surrounding Woodcleft Canal in Freeport—known to locals at the Nautical Mile—was the largest working waterfront on the south shore of Long Island at the end of the nineteenth century. The strip retains the flavor of a maritime community; it is a scenic boulevard lined with antique streetlamps, docks, boatyards, seafood restaurants, oyster bars, fish markets and popular saloons.

Today a diverse and densely populated community, Freeport and environs were settled by Dutch merchant traders in the mid-1600s and curate a colorful oceanic history that includes a one-time oyster industry and legends of smuggling and bootlegging. One can still find evidence of bay houses, small bungalows from where fishermen and baymen worked the surrounding waters each day. Convenient access to the Long Island Railroad during the early twentieth century prompted town fathers to promote Freeport as a seaside destination, and to encourage tourism, they dubbed the village the "Boating and Fishing Capital of the East" in the 1940s. Today, the area is a hub for commercial fishing fleets, charters, party boats and sun worshipers.

The Nautical Mile comes alive in the summer and is a popular destination for those craving sand, salt air and seafood. The Mile is notable

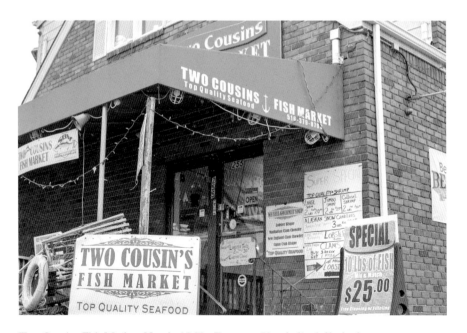

Two Cousins Fish Market, Nautical Mile, Freeport. *Photo by Jacob Skoglund.*

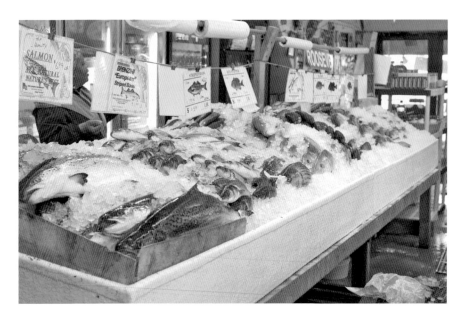

Catch of the day at Two Cousins Fish Market, Freeport. *Photo by Jacob Skoglund.*

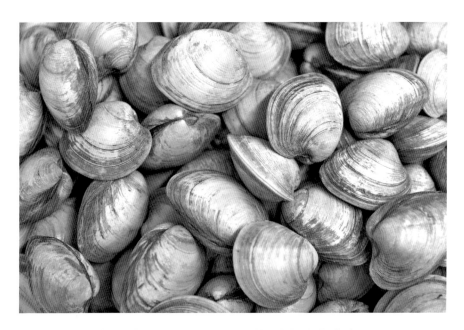

Local clams available on Freeport's Nautical Mile. *Photo by Jacob Skoglund.*

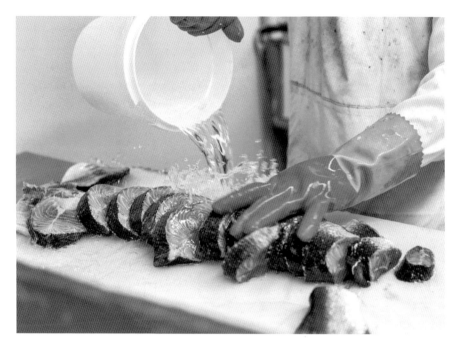

Fish is cleaned and filleted at Two Cousins Fish Market, Freeport. *Photo by Jacob Skoglund.*

for the long tenure of some of its restaurants. Otto's Sea Grill has operated for more than eighty-five years. The area took a beating when Hurricane Sandy struck the East Coast in October 2012. Some longtime restaurants and businesses were forced to close, but others fought back, rebuilt and reopened the following season.

The Nautical Mile is home to several classic fish markets where seafood-savvy Long Islanders arrive early to shop for the catch of the day. Captain Ben Bracco's Seafood Market is run by a second-generation "Miler" whose father first worked the waters as a commercial fisherman decades ago. Bracco's moved to a new, expanded location following Hurricane Sandy. Sadly, the Fiore Brothers Fish Market—the oldest on the strip and which had operated since 1946—was destroyed by an electrical fire the night Hurricane Sandy struck.

Two Cousins Fish Market sits alongside one of the only remaining commercial fishing docks on Woodcleft Avenue. A third-generation family business that began in the early 1930s, Two Cousins exudes the kind of old-time fishmonger atmosphere that has been erased from the modern supermarket seafood counter experience.

The air is sweet with the smell of the sea, and mountains of freshly caught local and imported seafood are piled high on ice in a large trough that runs along the center of the store. Lobster traps and nautical memorabilia hang from the ceiling. You'll discover a large live lobster tank at one end of the shop, and you'll likely marvel at the fact that the local oysters and clams seem impossibly large. Once you make a purchase, you can even take your fish to the back workroom, where the accommodating staff will clean and cut the fish to your specifications.

The Nautical Mile
Woodcleft Avenue
Freeport, NY, 11520
thenauticalmile.us

Two Cousins Fish Market
255 Woodcleft Avenue
Freeport, NY, 11520
516-379-0793
twocousins.com

Chapter 4
Preserving a Passion for Pickles

Most shoppers who thrill to the dill—craving the extensive choice of plump and pungent artisanal pickles available to them at Long Island farmers' markets—probably have no idea that Long Island was once a pickle paradise. From Syosset to Farmingdale to Greenlawn, pickle production was a boom business. In the late 1800s, at least six pickle factories operated in the town of Farmingdale alone.

The preponderance of pickles was the result of a convergence of cucumbers, manure and commerce. Cucumbers were a common crop for many central Long Island farmers. Manure was trucked in from New York City to supplement the sandy Long Island soil, producing a particularly robust cucumber. Pickling was an easy method to preserve the harvest. A typical brine solution might consist of salt, water, vinegar and spices. Cucumbers were layered with fresh herbs such as dill and garlic in a barrel or ceramic crock and submerged in a brine solution.

Farmers would ship their cucumbers to New York for brining, but soon "salting stations" started popping up on Long Island, often close to railroad stations to facilitate shipment of product to New York City. A farming journal speculated that a pickle grown in soil enriched with cow manure actually lasted longer. A post–Civil War influx of pickle-craving emigrants from Germany kept demand for pickles high. Thousands of Long Island–grown cucumbers were delivered to salting stations that operated in high gear from August through November. Uniformity was preferred, with pickles averaging three to four inches in length. Farmers could receive between two and four dollars per thousand pickles. Long Island was so prolific in pickle production that even the HJ Heinz Company—which had introduced its first brand of mass-produced pickles in 1893 at the Chicago World's Fair—got into the act and opened its own pickle factory in Hicksville in 1893.

Alart & McGuire was one of Long Island's largest processors, with pickle salting houses in Greenlawn, Syosett, Hicksville, Westbury, Deer Park, Riverhead and Mattituck. The Greenlawn-Centerport Historical Society has run an annual autumn Pickle Festival for nearly forty years—attended by thousands—celebrating that town's link to Long Island's pickle heritage.

Perhaps the most renowned enterprise was Stern's Pickle Works, notable for its longevity. Aaron Stern was an Austrian immigrant who sold pickles from a pushcart on Delaney Street on Manhattan's Lower East Side. He yearned for more and believed that he could make a better-quality pickle himself. Stern relocated to Long Island, where cucumbers were grown, and he purchased a pickle factory in Farmingdale. He opened for business in 1894. For several generations, the Stern family produced barrel-cured pickles brined in whiskey barrels. The pickles were prepared and packed by hand, using Aaron Stern's original recipe and no machinery. Stern's finally shut down in 1985, when the factory property was sold to developers.

Today, many artisans are preserving Long Island's pickle heritage.

PICKLE ME PETE

Pete Starr of Plainview has set up his wares at a local street fair, as he does most weekends. He wears a baseball cap in reverse and a black hoodie emblazoned with the emerald green slogan, "Keep Calm and Pickle On." White buckets brimming with chubby green pickles surround him.

A woman customer asks, "Do you have olives?" Starr doesn't miss a beat. "No," he answers politely. "If I did, I would be the Olive Man."

When you spend your days surrounded by pickles, you have to have a sense of humor, and there's no doubt that the jocular Starr views the world through pickle-colored glasses. In 2009, he ditched his job as an accountant for a life of brine. He founded Pickle Me Pete and never looked back, creating close to a dozen varieties of handcrafted, barrel-cured pickles that he sells at street fairs and festivals across Long Island and New York City. Starr is a postmodern Pickle Guy who embodies the entrepreneurial spirit of the Stern family yet embraces social media and the street food phenomenon.

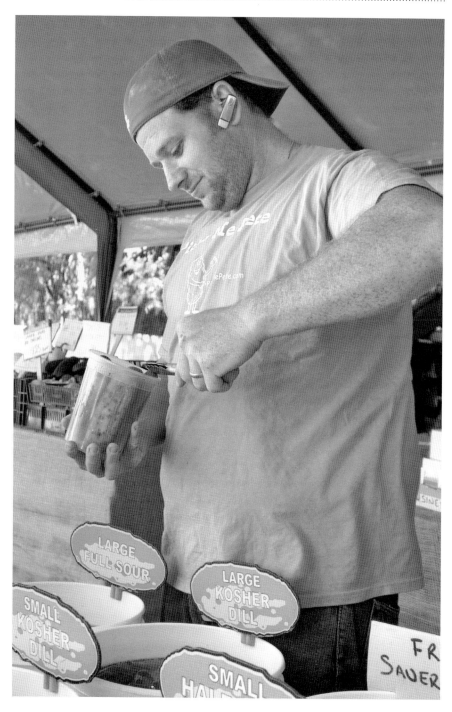

Former accountant Pete Starr founded the company Pickle Me Pete. *Photo by T.W. Barritt.*

A visit to Pickle Me Pete is a guarantee of fresh, crisp pickles served up with a smile and a bracing shot of Pickles 101. Starr works the barrels with gusto, drawing you into his emerald world. He also offers a wide range of theme-appropriate caps and T-shirts for the true pickle enthusiast.

Starr's recipes range from the traditional to the avant-garde. The self-proclaimed "Pickle Man" described his new half-sour pickle as a "confused cucumber." He also sells a pucker-worthy full sour pickle, kosher dills, sweet chipotle chips and varieties called "Super Spicy" and "Ridiculously Spicy," which are not for the faint of heart. Starr's fried pickles are a hot, tart and crunchy guilty pleasure.

For a flat delivery fee, the company also ships to Manhattan, Queens, Brooklyn, Nassau and Suffolk. In April 2015, Starr opened a brick-and-mortar store in Hicksville.

Pickle Me Pete
53 Bloomingdale Road
Hicksville, NY, 11801
516-531-3135
picklemepete.com

Horman's Best Pickles

Nick Horman Jr. is the heir to a Long Island pickle dynasty, and brine is in his blood. His family has been pickling for three generations, ever since his grandfather purchased a pickle cart in 1953 from Allen Pickle Works in Brooklyn. Horman's father, Nick Sr., got in on the business, too, and by 1992, the family had established a pickle factory in Glen Cove, Long Island, supplying to delis and supermarkets throughout the region. Nick Jr. worked in the plant, and armed with a BA in philosophy, he began an existential journey for pickle perfection. In 2003, he created his own artisan pickle business, which he dubbed Horman's Best Pickles.

Horman's propensity for philosophizing is evident in the company motto: "Think. Question. Pickle." Yet there's no debating the success of his venture. Given the humble asphalt origins of Horman's pickle pedigree, it was logical that he took his artisan pickles to the streets. Horman's Best Pickles are ubiquitous at open-air farmers' markets all over Long Island. One can easily spot the Horman's booth draped in mustard-colored banners emblazoned

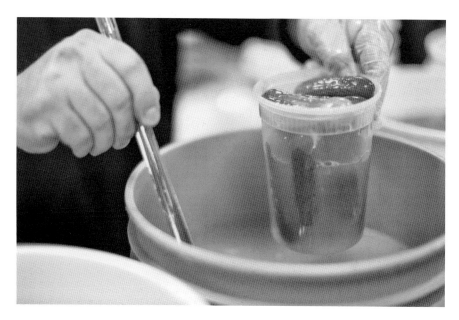

Horman's Best Pickles are a staple at farmers' markets on Long Island. *Photo by Jacob Skoglund.*

with pickle-green lettering. The barreled pickles glisten in the morning sun, and Horman's team of young pickle proselytizers stand ready to recruit a new convert.

Along with traditional varieties like kosher dill, new dill and bread and butter, Horman's offers several flavor-packed iconoclastic options, including sweet Cajun, honey mustard and red flannel.

Horman's Best Pickles
516-312-4726
hormansbestpickles.com

Chapter 5
Artisans and Entrepreneurs

From potato chips to Greek yogurt to specialty markets and online delivery services, Long Island's can-do spirit is evident in established business enterprises and an enthusiastic new breed of food artisans and entrepreneurs. When Long Islanders spot a niche, they tend to fill it, and some of the best food products and most durable businesses to emerge have sprung from family and ethnic traditions, backyard gardens, home kitchens and the fertile imaginations and dreams of determined individuals.

One can find businesses that endure through the decades, thanks to a reputation for unfailing customer service and strong community roots. Emerging businesses are often surprising and disruptive and are fundamentally changing the Long Island food scene, with business models and products and services never before seen. Collectively, these artisans and entrepreneurs set the standard for what it means to be "made on Long Island."

NORTH FORK POTATO CHIPS

At first glance, a glossy bag of North Fork Potato Chips might look like yet another high-end snack food. While noting the colorful, eye-catching packaging, you might actually miss the subtle, "S"-shaped logo at the center of the label. However, that logo is important, as it symbolizes the story of a Long Island farm family and a century spent cultivating the iconic Long

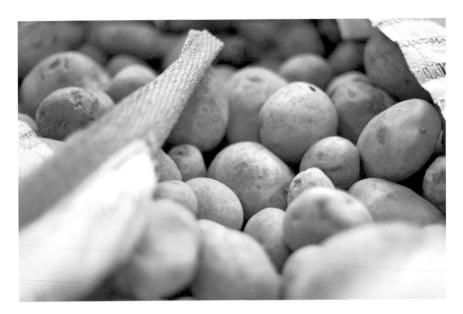

North Fork Potato Chips are made from the iconic Long Island potato. *Photo by Jacob Skoglund.*

Island potato. Martin Sidor Farms is one of a few remaining farm families that grows Long Island potatoes, and their modern potato chip company helps to keep that legacy alive.

Martin Sidor's grandfather emigrated from Poland in 1910 and settled in Mattituck on the North Fork of Long Island. There he grew potatoes, cabbage and cauliflower. He and his wife had four sons, all of whom went into farming. Martin Sidor is the son of the youngest of those four brothers. In college, he considered a career as a school psychologist but decided to return to the family homestead with his wife, Carol, to pursue a career in agriculture. Many of his peers were actually leaving their family farms and choosing other careers. This meant that many of the original potato farmers were retiring, and the land was being leased to sod growers or sold and replanted as vineyards. "Oregon Road in Cutchogue was full of one Polish-ancestry potato farmer after another, up until the 1970s," explained Carol Sidor.

The couple persevered, continuing to cultivate Long Island potatoes. The idea of launching a chip company emerged a little more than a decade ago from some creative brainstorming regarding the development of new revenue streams for the farm, but it wasn't as simple as it first sounded. "We said, 'Okay, how hard can it be?'" said Carol. "Famous last words!"

They began to investigate available equipment and manufacturing space. Just one piece of equipment was salvaged from an early purchase, but eventually the Sidors connected with a consultant who helped them purchase equipment from a chip factory in Wyoming. The machinery was loaded off the delivery truck on Independence Day weekend in 2003. "My first reaction was, 'Oh dear God. What did we do?'" said Carol.

It took about six months to assemble the machinery and become operational. Over the next ten years, the Sidors grew the business from the ground up, learning the ins and outs of production, packaging design and marketing. Today, Martin cultivates the potatoes in the fields, and Carol oversees all aspects of chip production at a leased facility in Cutchogue. About seventy-five acres of Martin Sidor Farms are used to grow "chipping potatoes."

Carol said that Long Island potatoes evoke a feeling of nostalgia for many, but the growing conditions on the North Fork also help ensure outstanding flavor. "It has a better taste because of the soil," she explained. "It grows a really good potato, and you get a great yield." Fans are surprised to learn that their favorite snack is connected to a local family farm, and Carol said that she enjoys educating people about the chips' backstory.

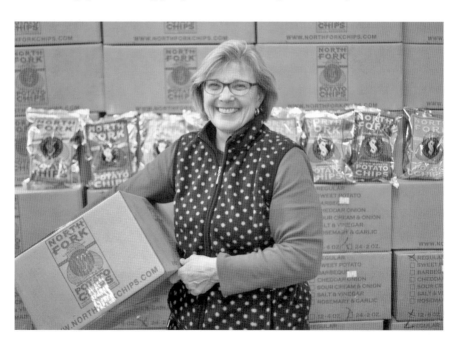

Carol Sidor of North Fork Potato Chips. *Photo by Jacob Skoglund.*

North Fork Potato Chips are kettle cooked in sunflower oil and are light and crisp with a sunny golden color. Varieties include original, barbeque, salt and vinegar, sweet potato, cheddar and onion, sour cream and onion and rosemary and garlic. A Long Island winery suggested that the Sidors create the rosemary and garlic flavor as a snack to pair with their local varieties of red wine.

Carol is the designated recipe developer for the company. "Our business meetings are at my kitchen table," she said. "If I like the flavor, we're going to do it."

The Sidors hope to expand their operation, and in early 2015, they were investigating construction of their own production facility, as well as a visitor museum devoted to the history of the Long Island potato.

North Fork Potato Chips
Martin Sidor Farms
Mattituck, Long Island, NY, 11952
631-734-2243
northforkchips.com

Farm2Kitchen Long Island

Former journalist Kassata Bollman created a new business model for people who appreciate local, sustainably grown food but might not have the time, inclination or ability to trudge to a farmers' market. In May 2013, the North Fork resident launched Farm2Kitchen Long Island, an online farmers' market, promising to build stronger bonds between busy Long Islanders and local farmers and artisans. "It all comes down to connections," said Bollman. "That's the number one word that describes our company."

Bollman crowd-sourced funding for Farm2Kitchen Long Island through an online campaign, which pitched the weekly home delivery service as a way to extend the reach of local farmers and artisans to the broader community.

Farm2Kitchen provides weekly home delivery to residents of Long Island in Nassau and Suffolk Counties, as well as the Bronx, Brooklyn, Manhattan, Queens and Staten Island. Customers create an online account and can select delivery to home or office. The service requires a forty-dollar minimum order and includes a delivery fee. Orders must be placed by midnight Saturday for

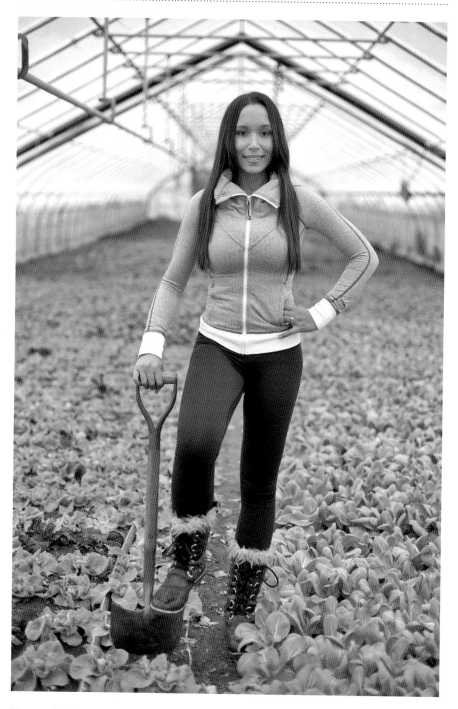

Kassata Bollman founded the online marketplace Farm2Kitchen Long Island. *Photo by Jacob Skoglund.*

delivery the following week. Fresh food is delivered in insulated totes and pouches packed with dry ice.

Farm2Kitchen offers a hybrid of convenience and conviction. Determined to follow through on her vision to fundamentally change the dynamic in the local food economy, Bollman acts as a virtual curator of the best of the bounty of Long Island for people who want to know exactly from where their food comes. The online market offers organic and biodynamic produce, baked goods, beverages, bread, chocolate, dairy, fresh herbs, meat, poultry and meal kits. Special orders are available for holidays, as are winter shares of organic produce. Bollman's network of producers includes long-established entities such as Sang Lee Farms, Lewin Farms and Wickham's Fruit Farm, as well as a full range of specialty products. She also sources from producers in other areas within New York State.

Bollman launched with ten customers and, after a year of operating, had increased to nearly one thousand. "They hug me and thank me when I meet them," said Bollman. "What all of these people have in common is a desire to support local farmers, and we're their connection to them."

Bollman is more than simply a connector of healthy and nutritious food. Her skills as a storyteller emerge in all aspects of Farm2Kitchen's interactions with customers, and she uses those skills to build relationships between her far-flung customers and her suppliers. Individual products contain inserts describing the farm or food purveyor, their history and philosophy. The website marketplace includes a profile of each participating company.

Farm2Kitchen Long Island
PO Box 743
Southold, NY, 11971
631-223-8854
farm2kitchenlongisland.com

A TASTE OF LONG ISLAND
SPECIALTY MARKET AND KITCHEN

A storefront on Main Street in Farmingdale is providing aspiring Long Island food entrepreneurs with a head start to launch their businesses. Father and daughter founders Jim Thompson and Courtney Citko established A Taste of Long Island in 2012 as a private-use commercial kitchen and specialty

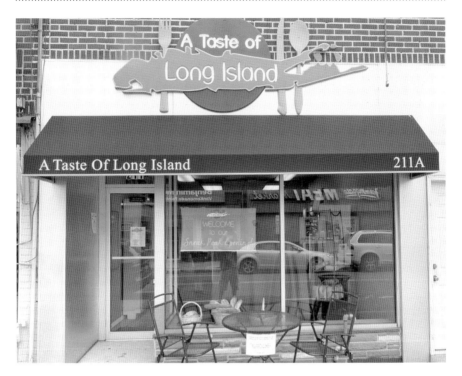

A Taste of Long Island Specialty Market in Farmingdale only sells products made on Long Island. *Photo by T.W. Barritt.*

food market. Thompson sees their kitchen incubator and specialty market as a small business whose mission is to help other small businesses expand.

Food products produced for sale or resale in New York State must be prepared in a commercial kitchen that complies with all local health and safety codes. Recognizing that most food businesses start off in a home kitchen but require scale and permits to expand, Thompson and Citko designed and built an eight-hundred-square-foot commercial kitchen that meets all Good Manufacturing Practices and is available to clients around the clock to rent on an hourly basis. Equipment includes professional gas ranges and ovens, stand mixers, food preparation tables, bake ware, utensils and a refrigerator and freezer. A Taste of Long Island also offers small business training and advice to clients looking to establish their business and brand.

A Taste of Long Island offers a one-stop shop for product manufacturing and marketing. Clients can produce batches of product in the rental kitchen and actually arrange for space in the storefront food market to sell product. For food entrepreneurs just starting out, the food market is often their first regular exposure to the public. The store resembles a diverse gourmet shop merged with a hometown bakery and offers a large selection of custom-made cakes and cookies, pickles, granola, chutneys, French macarons, salad dressings, salsas, specialty breads, pasta, tea and coffee crafted by Long Island food artisans. Patrons are regularly treated to tastings of Long Island wines.

"We're proud that we've assisted in the launch of numerous food-preneurs on Long Island," said Thompson. "By providing basic business startup direction, guidance on meeting regulatory requirements and a first distribution channel for companies to sell their products through our specialty food store and farmers' markets, we believe we're making a very positive contribution to the local Long Island economy."

In 2014, the enterprise expanded its incubator business model to open A Taste of Long Island Craft Brewery. Now officially licensed as a New York State farm brewery, A Taste of Long Island pours Thompson's flagship beer, Farmingdale Natural Blonde Ale. The commercial kitchen is also open to aspiring microbrewers to ferment, package and distribute their product.

A Taste of Long Island Specialty Market and Kitchen
211-A Main Street
Farmingdale, NY, 11735
516-694-2859
atasteoflongislandny.com

KALYPSO GREEK YOGURT

Like many immigrant families, Nick Trastelis's Greek forefathers brought agricultural and culinary traditions from their homeland when they arrived in the United States and settled throughout New York and Long Island. Trastelis said that Greek yogurt was always at the center of his family. "It started with my great-granddad back in the old country," explained the native of Brooklyn and Huntington, Long Island. "He had migrated through Ellis Island, set up business a couple of blocks just south of Macy's in Herald Square and opened a little dairy shop making the yogurt I grew up on."

Trastelis remembers straining Greek yogurt during summers as a youngster at his grandparents' home in the Greek countryside, but the activity might not have had the romantic connotations or business implications it has for him today. He would herd the goats, milk them and bring the milk

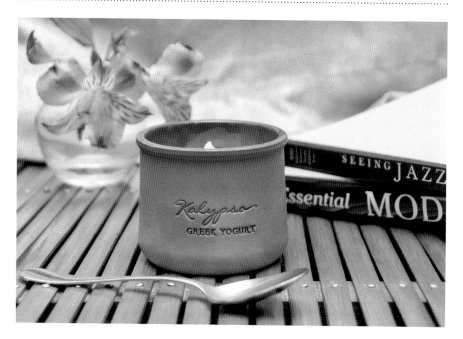

Kalypso Greek Yogurt, in its distinctive terra-cotta cup. *Photo by Lucia Cascio, courtesy of Kalypso Greek Yogurt.*

pails back to the farmstead to begin the process of straining yogurt in little muslin bags with his grandmother. "It was a nightmare," Trastelis laughed. "I remember being eight or nine years old, and the last thing I wanted to do was milk a goat." He described his grandparents' town of Karpenisi as "an obscure Greek village known for its dairy and charcuterie."

Trastelis perhaps never imagined that he would one day become the founder of a company that markets Greek yogurt. The distinctive, earth-tone terra-cotta pots that contain Trastelis's luscious Kalypso Greek Yogurt have inspired a cult following at Long Island farmers' markets from Long Beach to Southampton. "It's in our fabric, and it's what we always did," said Trastelis. "I went full circle, and here I am crafting Greek yogurt again."

Trastelis's family has run a local food service business for four generations. He worked in New York finance and other businesses for nearly two decades before embarking on a cultural food odyssey that took him back to his native land. He was dismayed by commercial products claiming to be authentic Greek yogurt and visited Greek islands, villages and rural areas, collecting family recipes and eventually landing on the recipe that is now Kalypso Greek Yogurt. "With Kalypso, I wanted to bring back our culture and our

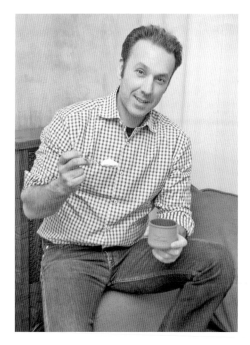

Nick Trastelis created Kalypso Greek Yogurt based on a family recipe. *Photo by Lucia Cascio, courtesy of Kalypso Greek Yogurt.*

roots and reclaim what Greek yogurt is," he noted.

The terra-cotta pots are the traditional serving vessel for yogurt in Greece, as the porous material helps to drain the whey from the yogurt. Trastelis brought the tradition to Long Island, launching the yogurt line in greenmarkets throughout Nassau and Suffolk. Inside each container is a perfect, seductive dollop of thick, creamy Greek yogurt. The terra-cotta packaging makes an environmental statement, as the clay vessels are 100 percent recyclable. They also inspire the imagination of customers, who reuse the pots for everything from candleholders to muffin cups to planters.

Kalypso Greek Yogurt is available in nonfat flavors that include honey, black cherry, strawberry, vanilla, blueberry, fig and plain. Trastelis experiments with small-batch varieties and also introduced toasted coconut and lemon fennel varieties.

The fruit-on-the-bottom flavors are based on a Greek tradition called "spoon sweets." Trastelis said that a Greek family throws nothing away and that small bits of fruit or vegetables will be cooked down and reduced into a rich, gelatinous preserve. The preserves are served to guests on spoons and are a symbol of Greek hospitality.

Kalypso is expanding into several retail and gourmet markets in the New York area, but Trastelis said that the farmers' markets will always be home. "We'll never give up the markets because that's where we started," he explained. "We use the markets as a sounding board to get instant feedback from our fans. To be able to craft something with your hands and then have the feedback of someone enjoying what you're actually making is an amazing feeling."

Kalypso Greek Yogurt
kalypsoyogurt.com

North Fork Sea Salt Company

Scott Bollman's connection to the North Fork—and the ocean that surrounds it—inspired a business that he hopes will get people thinking about the food they eat and the ingredients available around them. The Southold native started North Fork Sea Salt Company in September 2012—harvesting sea salt from East End waters—and markets the handcrafted product to restaurant chefs, retail establishments and home cooks. The artisanal sea salt is available in two- and four-ounce jars.

As a trained chef, Bollman knows the importance of salt as a flavor enhancer and preservative. "Salt is the most utilized ingredient in the kitchen," he said. "To source it locally is a huge step to creating a sustainable menu."

He described the finishing salt as briny and delicate. Bollman attended culinary school in New York City and eventually migrated back to Southold. "The North Fork was becoming a food destination and a chef-driven area," he explained.

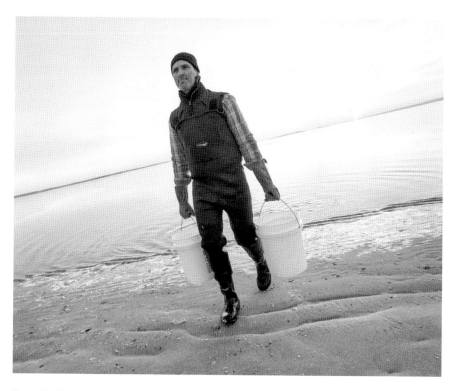

Scott Bollman gathers ocean water to produce North Fork Sea Salt. *Photo courtesy Randee Daddona.*

Harvesting artisanal sea salt was a logical extension of his culinary training and his roots. "You can't grow up out here without being involved with water. That passion is what started me on this journey—the passion of being a local and loving the area."

To craft the sea salt, Bollman harvests from calm waters on the shoreline of the Long Island Sound in the summer months and the Great Peconic Bay in winter months. He said that the location of the water influences the taste of the salt. "We've harvested all over the East End, from the ocean tide to the bay, and we have these little spots," he explained. "You can tell the difference, from the taste, to the temperature, to the crystal size."

Bollman creates a concentrated brine that forms salt crystals at low temperatures. Just like snowflakes, every salt crystal extracted is different, and the resulting taste evokes the strong connection Long Islanders have to the sea. "It's a nostalgia flavor," he explained. "Anybody that's grown up out here has swallowed some seawater or took some water up the nose. It takes you back. There's something about the sweetness and the brininess of the water out here that you can taste in the salt. It triggers something in your brain that relates to knowing the waters out here."

Bollman focuses on simplicity, offering a plain version of the local sea salt and just a few varieties that he described as "farm stand blends." For a smoked salt, he burns grapevines from a local winery. The flavor for his heirloom tomato salt is drawn from tomatoes raised at a local farm that employs biodynamic growing practices. "Whatever's on the farm stand, or whatever's local and in our radius, we use to flavor our salt," he explained.

Bollman noted that North Fork Sea Salt Company is about preserving the unique sense of place and flavor found on the East End of Long Island. "It's about just being connected and sharing that connection with other people—chefs, home cooks and anybody that's interested or wants to be educated about knowing where their food comes from."

North Fork Sea Salt Company
631-209-SALT
northforkseasaltco.com

Georgio's Coffee Roasters

An unassuming storefront in Farmingdale conceals a high-octane hub of international coffee sourcing. Georgio Testani and his wife, Lydia, have been in the coffee sourcing and roasting business for nearly twenty-five years, but if you're looking for Wi-Fi and pound cake, you should look elsewhere. At Georgio's Coffee Roasters, there are no frilly extras—just a selection of the highest-quality coffee beans sourced from top markets all over the world. "We don't do a million lattes and cappuccinos," said Georgio. "Every other coffee house does that. You won't see any French vanilla coffee here and no hazelnut. I just don't want to do it."

The store is part laboratory, part warehouse and part roasting facility, and the couple is clearly driven by a deep passion for coffee and a commitment to perfection. The Testanis travel the world in search of the best coffee beans. Their customers range from individual coffee aficionados who stream in during the day to national coffee companies looking to up their game. Georgio's sells twenty-two single-origin coffees and ships products to forty states and seven countries. The couple has visited six coffee-producing countries and more than sixty farms in regions that include Colombia, Brazil,

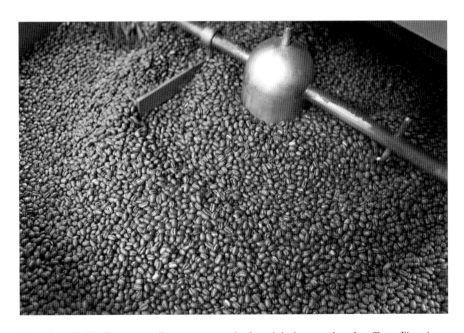

Georgio's Coffee Roasters sells twenty-two single-origin international coffees. *Photo by Jacob Skoglund.*

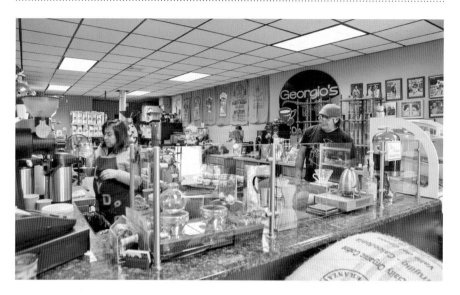

Georgio's Coffee Roasters is part laboratory, part warehouse and part roasting facility. *Photo by Jacob Skoglund.*

El Salvador and East Africa. He estimated that on some weeks they move nearly eight thousand pounds of coffee through the Farmingdale store. "We have the rarest list of coffees in the world," said Georgio.

If you are lucky enough to catch Georgio at work, you might observe him roasting coffee beans in a German roaster or cupping coffee, a tasting process in which he and his wife sample the flavors and aromas of a particular bean around a circular table. It requires using the senses of sight, smell and taste to assess the quality of a coffee bean. Watching the two slurp and inhale the complex coffee aromas is mesmerizing. "Coffee is theater," he admitted.

The Testanis have a deep commitment to coffee farmers and strive to offer producers a fair price. "We don't care how much it costs," said Georgio. "We want the top farms in the world."

Georgio's Coffee Roasters
1965 New Highway
Farmingdale, NY, 11735
516-238-2999
georgioscoffee.com

Chapter 6
Curds and Whey

As a youngster, the only cow I'd ever seen was a live version of "Elsie"—the fetching bovine cartoon mascot of the Borden Dairy Company—at the 1964 World's Fair. I was well into adulthood before I'd even heard of or tasted goat cheese. That bracingly fresh, tangy, grassy flavor was an earthly delight still waiting to be discovered. My framework for cheese was simple. It was "American," it came from the grocery store, it was individually wrapped in cellophane and the color was a bright school bus yellow.

Artisan cheese on Long Island is a bit of a rare commodity. You have to look hard. An actual dairy is tough to come by. And you need a dairy to produce milk in order to make cheese.

My family's perception of a dairy was somewhat skewed by a growing convenience store mentality. Our suburban landscape was dotted with bright red drive-thru "Dairy Barns," each complete with a towering silo. It was an oddly bucolic vision on the typical Long Island highway (which often sported a 7-Eleven, a McDonald's boasting millions and millions served and the odd assortment of playgrounds, firehouses and professional office buildings).

The Dairy Barn was part of our weekly routine. Piled into the family station wagon returning from Sunday church services, we would approach the Dairy Barn via a driveway on either side of the structure. An attendant would lean out, and we'd place an order—usually for a half gallon of milk, a dozen eggs and perhaps some ice cream as the finale for our Sunday dinner. The attendant would pass the order through the window, we'd pay cash and we'd be on our way.

What we didn't know was that our local Dairy Barn was the outpost for an actual Long Island dairy. In 1939, Dieter Cosman had taken over management of his father Edgar's ailing dairy farm, Oak Tree Farm Dairy, in the town of Elwood in Suffolk County. By the late 1940s, the farm was financially healthy, supported by a strong wholesale milk business and home milk deliveries. By the late 1950s, however, preferences had shifted, and the home delivery business was in decline. Cosman needed a new business model to offer milk to the masses, and he opened the first Dairy Barn convenience store in 1961 to service the increasingly mobile Long Island resident. Oak Tree Farm Dairy was a family-owned operation well into the twenty-first century, although the dairy cows eventually relocated to upstate New York and the site was later run exclusively as a milk packaging and distribution facility. Sadly, for those of us who love suburban nostalgia, the number of Dairy Barns has since dwindled dramatically to a small handful.

So what's this got to do with cheese? Milk and cheese go together. Cheese is a happy byproduct of milk and a way to extend the value of surplus milk. Oak Tree Farm Dairy billed itself as Long Island's only dairy, but it focused on fluid milk production—the claim was, perhaps, marketing hyperbole. There are likely many examples of Long Island families who would have kept a cow or a goat and made cheese from surplus milk produced on the farm. If milk was plentiful, cheese was inevitable, but it was more a matter of frugality than of culinary art. The dairy was an important component of a family estate. The Bayard Cutting Arboretum in Great River includes a historic barn where the William Bayard Cutting family kept a herd of Jersey milking cows. At Caumsett State Park in Lloyds Neck, one can view an extensive dairy operation that was once part of the former Marshall Field estate. There is also evidence of small local dairies. In the early part of the twentieth century, William H. Pierson and a partner operated the Suffolk Dairy in Water Mill. Pierson kept about sixty milking cows and shipped chilled cream by train to New York City.

Producing artisan cheese is far more than a hobby and requires an understanding of animal husbandry and a significant physical, monetary and emotional investment. Today, a cheese maker must be willing to care for the herd and have the skills and temperament to handcraft a distinctive cheese whose flavors evoke the characteristics of the region. New York State is one of the top milk producers in the nation and a major producer of cottage cheese, sour cream and Italian cheese. Long Island cheese, however, is a work in progress yet making great strides on both the North and South Forks. Several trailblazers are managing large herds and defining the terroir of cheese on the East End. The curious cheese enthusiast can find everything from award-winning goat cheese to exquisite French-style raw milk cheeses. And if you can't get to the dairies, several expert cheese purveyors can help you out.

Catapano Dairy Farm

The reaction is almost always the same. People who know it seem to swoon visibly at the mention of Catapano Farm Fresh Goat Cheese from the picturesque Catapano Dairy Farm in Peconic. Enter the driveway off North Road and you'll encounter a charming periwinkle-blue cottage stocked with fresh goat cheese and beauty products made from pure goat milk. Just beyond, happy goats are frolicking around a replica of Noah's ark. Lean close to the fence and you'll almost swear the goats are smiling at you.

Karen Catapano, a former critical care nurse who started the dairy with her physician husband, Michael, in 2003, is a slender, vivacious woman who is clearly passionate about the work they do. She said that the public response to their product can be attributed to flavor and familiarity. "It's the taste. It's delicious. People in America don't know how good goat cheese is and don't realize how good it's supposed to taste. It's supposed to have that very fresh, clean taste."

The dairy welcomes visitors, and it's not unusual to see parents with young children stopping by to purchase cheese and spend some time socializing with the goats. Although flanked by a large milking and production shed, there is a pastoral feel to the tidy, well-manicured farm. Indeed, as one of the only cheese making operations on Long Island (that is also open to the public), Catapano Dairy has become part of the fabric of the North Fork community. Karen described it as part agritourism and part education. "A lot of people have been here, so they get to know where their cheese came from. They get to know the goats. They know they can trust us because they've been here, they've seen how clean it is and they can see the animals."

While the idea of buying a farm and making cheese sounds romantic, Karen affirmed that the year-round effort is hard work, something they learned from the outset. "It's a huge undertaking—that's the only thing I can say," she said. "There's no template. You have to understand the process start to finish and then back it up and create your plan and how you want it

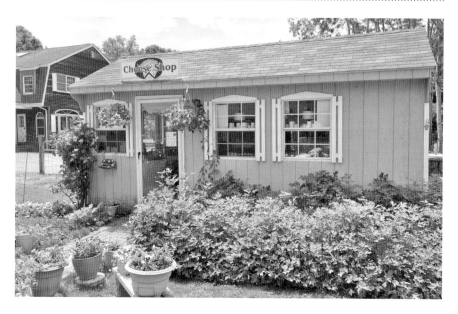

Catapano Dairy Farm in Peconic is Long Island's premier producer of goat cheese. *Photo by T.W. Barritt.*

to work for you. And you have to be smart enough and dedicated enough to set it up right to begin with and then stay with it."

Starting out, the couple bought a smaller farm in Mattituck in 2003, just after their son was deployed to Iraq. The previous owners had struggled with the amount of time and money needed to make the business viable. "The opportunity came, we needed something in our lives to do and we took a risk and did it," said Karen. They purchased the farm in less than a week, and they began to educate themselves, studying animal care and cheese making on a dairy in upstate New York. They established their own operation, and Michael immersed himself in the art of cheese making. In 2005, Catapano Chèvre Cheese was named best goat cheese in the United States by the American Cheese Society. As word of the award spread, they could no longer keep the chèvre in stock and made the decision to move to a larger plot of land in Peconic and expand their operation in 2006.

The Catapanos have kept up to six of the major breeds of dairy goats, including Saanen, Alpine, Nubian, LaMancha, Oberhasli and Toggenburg. Today, much of their focus is on the Saanen breed, as well as a Saanen and Alpine mix. They manage a herd of up to one hundred goats at a time. Karen said that the care and feeding of the goats has the greatest influence on taste and quality. "When they're happy and they're healthy, that makes me feel like everything is working and we're all doing the right things," she said.

Catapano Dairy Farm produces several styles of goat cheese, which it sells at its cheese shop and markets to restaurants, wineries and farm stands throughout the area. One will often find Catapano cheese listed on the menus of the finest restaurants of the North and South Forks. Its signature, creamy white chèvres are soft cheeses, several flavored with local garlic, horseradish or honey. The feta cheese is a semi-dry cheese pressed in a mold. The dairy also features several aged cheeses. Summer Cloud is a farmstead-aged goat cheese, and Sundancer is a farmstead-aged goat/sheep cheese. Other offerings include ricotta and yogurt. Peconic Belle, a four-week aged sheep cheese, was released in 2015. Catapano Dairy continues to earn accolades and was awarded Best Cheese in 2008, 2009 and 2013 by the American Cheese Society.

Karen also sells a line of skin care products called the Delicate Doe, which features premium goat milk soap, bath bars and face creams. Goat milk nourishes the skin and has excellent moisturizing qualities.

At one point several years ago—due to the demands of Michael's medical practice—the Catapanos considered a lifestyle change and put the dairy up for sale. They were clear that the dairy had to be sold intact, but according to Karen, none of the potential buyers wanted to take on the work of a day-to-day operation. So the couple reevaluated and made several staff hires to help run the dairy. "We figured it out," said Karen. "And I'm so glad it worked out that way."

Catapano Dairy Farm
33705 North Road
Peconic, NY, 11958
631-765-8042
catapanodairyfarm.com

The Big Cheese

Mark Cassin cuts an imposing figure. The self-appointed "Big Cheese" is indeed a towering, bear of a guy whose stock in trade is dairy's most delicious derivative. A roving cheese monger who works the Long Island farmers' markets and organizes tasting events, Cassin is perhaps the most enthusiastic booster around for cheese produced in New York State.

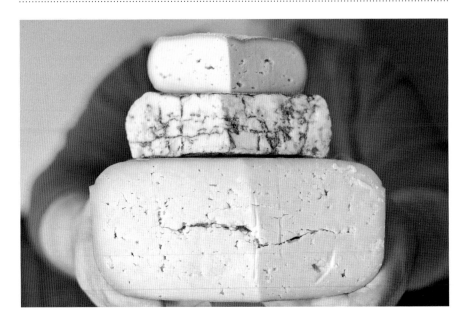

Cheese monger Mark Cassin is known as the "Big Cheese." *Photo by Jacob Skoglund.*

Some years ago, Cassin was considering starting a food business and noted the dearth of cheese venues on Long Island. "I realized that living in Sag Harbor, we used to have a really great cheese shop," he said. "I knew there were great shops in Brooklyn, but there was nothing in our area. My idea was to open a cheese shop somewhere central on Long Island."

A cheese making stint at Mecox Bay Dairy solidified Cassin's plan, but with a slight twist. He decided to eschew brick and mortar and take his campaign directly to the people. "I started to sell cheese at different farmers' markets," said Cassin. "I was going to do all domestic cheeses, and I realized that was being done, so I decided to take it a step further and do 100 percent New York State cheeses."

The Big Cheese is easily spotted at farmers' markets from Long Beach to Northport. His portable glass display case highlights eight to ten cheeses at a time, so it's easy for shoppers to see his product and understand the story of each dairy involved. Cassin likes the opportunity to interact with customers. "There's a lot of dairy going on in New York, and people are trying to get value-added product out of a gallon of milk," said Cassin. "I'm able to have a one-on-one with people to discuss the farms." He particularly enjoys the interaction with younger patrons. "The kids are fearless," said Cassin. "They go for the craziest stuff that I have in the boxes. The fun part is to watch kids really gobble this stuff up."

Cassin also organizes cheese pairings at Long Island wineries and craft breweries and is finding infinite opportunities to demonstrate the pleasures of cheese from New York State, where dairy is experiencing a renaissance. "They're all working together," he said of the New York State cheese producers. "All the dairies are talking to each other, and great cheese makers are counseling others at smaller dairies, helping them and answering their questions. It's rebuilding the dairy industry."

Cassin is humbled that he plays a part in spreading the good news about local cheese across Long Island. He has created a new market for New York State cheese makers who might otherwise never get their product to Long Island, and he is particularly gratified when one of his upstate farmers hears from a satisfied customer who first sampled their product from the Big Cheese. "That's a beautiful thing," he said. "That's what makes it worth it."

The Big Cheese (Mark Cassin)
516-315-1048
thebigcheeseny.com

Bruce & Son Cheese Emporium and Café

Bruce Bollman had no experience running a cheese shop when he opened the North Fork's first gourmet cheese emporium in Greenport in 1974. His wife suggested the idea casually while paging through a magazine. "I said, I don't know anything about cheese," recalled Bollman. "I grew up on Velveeta and American cheese."

Yet the couple did their research and got the venture up and running. The early days of the shop were humble beginnings, according to Bollman. "I opened in two hundred square feet. It was like a walk-in closet."

Bollman's mother predicted ominously that the shop wouldn't last a year. Yet the idea proved to be fortuitous. A year earlier, Louisa and Alex Hargrave had planted Long Island's first vineyard in Cutchogue, and interest in local wines and artisanal products was beginning to take root. "When you think of it, I was the first cheese shop, and they were the first winery," said Bollman. "Now we have some forty wineries, so over the years I've seen a lot of change."

Today, the business is at its third location in Greenport and has evolved but retains a certain small-town charm. The walls are hung with black-and-white photos of old Greenport, and an embossed white tin ceiling frames the interior. Bollman offers 125 varieties of cheese, and over time the café was added. Bollman's son, Scott, who also owns the North Fork Sea Salt Company, is chef, and he can be spotted in the back kitchen cooking up hearty omelets with cheese and decadent sandwiches, including a creation layered with prosciutto, cheese and fig jam known as the Pig n Fig. What's the secret to their longevity?

"We change with the times, of course," Bollman replied.

Bruce & Son Cheese Emporium and Café
208 Main Street
Greenport, NY, 11944
631-477-0023
brucescheeseemp.com

MECOX BAY DAIRY

It is milking time at Mecox Bay Dairy in Bridgehampton. Six Jersey cows are lined up in the milking room in midafternoon, joined to a noisy milking machine. Owner and cheese maker Art Ludlow strokes the nose of one of the girls. "Jersey cows are well suited for artisanal cheeses," he said with a smile. "Their milk has a high fat content and high protein, and they're also pretty cows."

It's an endearing comment from a man who said he started making aged, raw milk cheeses as a creative enterprise nearly fifteen years ago in an effort to diversify his South Fork family farm. "Cheese from the store—Kraft singles and all that stuff—that's generic, that's processed," said Ludlow. "There is a flavor that can be unlocked by making cheese on the farm. There's a lot of terroir involved, and so I thought, 'Nobody's making cheese out here. What's it going to taste like? What would it be like?'"

Ludlow's journey to find that answer reflects the progression of his family farm. It is the story of an agricultural enterprise that has evolved with the times.

Ludlow already had a deep, familial connection to the land. His father's grandfather purchased ten acres of property—now part of the modern-day Bridgehampton farm—in 1875. Together with a brother, he did subsistence farming, caught oysters and soft-shell crabs in the bay and worked as a caretaker on a nearby estate. Ludlow's grandfather was the first to farm the land full time around 1919 and expanded the property to about eighty acres. "He grew potatoes and had a dairy farm," said Ludlow. "My grandfather never farmed with a tractor. He farmed with horses his entire time."

Ludlow's grandfather died of blood poisoning at a young age after an accident with a piece of farm equipment. Ludlow's father took on responsibility for the farm as a teenager and continued operating the dairy and growing potatoes until 1959. By that time, milk prices had dropped, so the family made the decision to eliminate the dairy and focus on potatoes. Ludlow and his brother attended Cornell College of Agriculture and continued farming the family land, leasing additional acreage to grow potatoes. By the year 2000, the economic environment had changed again. They were shipping their commercial potato crop to New York City and as far as South Carolina and Puerto Rico, but increasingly, there was less land available in the area to grow crops and sustain their business, so the family had to consider a new direction for the farm. "We thought if our kids wanted to farm, there's not going to be enough land to increase the acreage and farm potatoes," said Ludlow. "So we decided in 2000 that would be the last year we grew potatoes."

Ludlow explained that they refocused their efforts locally. "We have a great, long growing season, we have good soils and we have a market at our back door, so why not grow something that doesn't have to be shipped somewhere?" His brother decided to grow vegetables, but Ludlow chose a different direction.

Mecox Road in Bridgehampton meanders along the edge of palatial estates before reaching the Ludlow farm. A dairy seems like an anachronism in a district of Bridgehampton devoted to exclusive summer getaways. Age-old shade trees conceal the Ludlow homestead, Jersey cows graze in the adjacent field and turkeys wander the property.

Sitting at the dining room table in his family's ancestral farmhouse, Ludlow is thoughtful and deliberate about his transformation from potato farmer to artisan cheese maker. "I've always liked cows, and I liked the idea of making cheese. It's a creative type of thing. My idea was—it's a small farm—I can make cheese and sell it locally and not have to get into a long-range distribution issue. And in so doing, I thought it was best if I made a variety of styles of cheeses."

In a visual sign of the farm's evolution, the dairy—built by Ludlow—is housed within the shell of the former potato barn. A series of continuous chambers include the milking room, the bulk tank room, the cheese making room and the aging room. In the aging room, there are dozens upon dozens of rounds of cheese stacked on shelves from floor to ceiling. The yeasty, ripe aroma is heady, to say the least.

Mecox Bay Dairy cheeses are the very essence of a local Long Island product. About 80 percent of the cheese produced is sold within a forty-mile radius, and Ludlow sells primarily through farm stands and farmers' markets. All are raw milk cheeses, which means the milk is not treated in any way. Perennial favorites include soft ripened cheeses, washed rind cheeses, moderate-flavored cheeses, Alpine-style cheeses and cheddars, all with romantically evocative names like Mecox Sunrise, Atlantic Mist, Sigit and the natural rind Tomme called Shawondasee, a Native American word that means "southwest wind." Ludlow said that he has the flexibility to experiment and try new things. "In the United States, we didn't have a history of developing unique cheeses like you find in other places. It was whatever was brought from the Old World. I'm not constrained to making certain cheeses. I'm not living in Camembert, where I have to make Camembert. I can do whatever I want."

He is strict about the cows' diet and made the decision not to use fermented feed, as it would affect the flavor of the milk. In 2015, the Ludlows were milking twelve Jersey cows. The herd is fed hay, some grain and grass from the pastures. Ludlow's son, Peter, returned to the farm after college and is exploring ways to grow more of the feed on the farm.

Over time, this very local product has garnered more attention, and Ludlow is looking to expand the business to western Long Island and New York City. "I still like the creative aspect of it both from the standpoint of producing a cheese but also the challenge to create a business that is going to be sustainable," he explained.

It is all part of the evolution that began when the Ludlow family farm was first established in the late nineteenth century. "It's still a work in progress," said Ludlow of his artisan cheese enterprise. "But I'm learning all the time and constantly trying to tweak things." Through it all, he is confident of the quality of the cheeses made at Mecox Bay Dairy. "If you're doing something that's free of meddling, that's natural, it has to taste good."

Mecox Bay Dairy
855 Mecox Road
Bridgehampton, NY, 11932
631-537-0335

Chapter 7
Daily Bread

Bread is one of the oldest sources of nutrition known to the human race. Grain and bread on Long Island have nourished the family, fed the expansion of an agrarian society and given rise to everything from family businesses to large commercial enterprises.

In the 1960s—for better or worse—bread on Long Island was white and squishy and usually came in a plastic bag. The CBS children's television host Captain Kangaroo (who hailed from Lynbrook, Long Island) would tell young viewers like me to look for Wonder Bread in the grocery store, with the red, yellow and blue balloons printed on the package. The commercially produced sliced bread was considered a modern-day marvel. Baked with refined flour and enriched with vitamins and minerals, Wonder Bread promised to build "strong bodies 8 ways." It must have been regarded as a "super food" by parents hoping to raise the perfect child.

An unwitting casualty of early efforts to market to children, I found the visual image of the colorful balloons captivating, and I desperately wanted Wonder Bread. Our family's flirtation with squishy white bread lasted just until I was too old for Captain Kangaroo and my mother discovered the more healthful, fiber-filled varieties of whole wheat bread that were beginning to enter the commercial market.

Well before Long Islanders craved efficiency and convenience, bread was a dietary staple. Native Americans ground corn into meal and baked corn bread in flat disks on rocks heated by open fires. European settlers were accustomed to grains such as wheat and rye but learned from Native

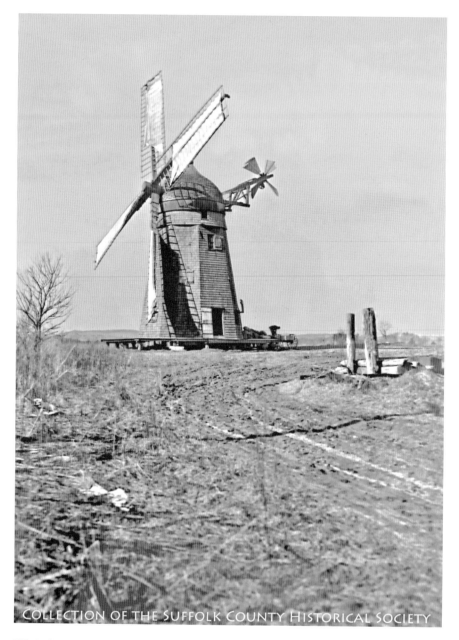

Windmill, Bridgehampton, New York, circa 1899, by Hal B. Fullerton. *From the Harry T. Tuthill Fullerton Collection of the Suffolk County Historical Society. Copyright © Suffolk County Historical Society. All rights reserved.*

Americans how to grow corn and cook with cornmeal. They baked bread in brick or stone ovens located near the central fireplace in a household kitchen. Long Island food historian Alice Ross has written extensively about hearth cooking and shared recipes for corn bread baked in Dutch ovens or three-legged "spider" frying pans that were placed in the hot ashes of the hearth.

As agricultural operations expanded across Long Island and more farmers planted grains, they needed additional resources to effectively utilize and monetize the harvest. Beginning in 1644, a network of windmills was built that—in addition to sawing wood and pumping water—served as local centers where farmers could bring grain and have it ground into flour. Eleven historic wooden windmills can still be found throughout Suffolk County today. Other evidence of the infrastructure that sprang up in service of daily bread includes the still-standing Saddle Rock Grist Mill in the village of Great Neck. Built in about 1700, it is one of the oldest tidal gristmills in the United States. The Stony Brook Grist Mill, built about 1751, supported farmers looking to grind wheat and corn as recently as the 1940s. Visitors to Blydenburgh County Park in Smithtown can view a historic milling center established in 1798 by the Smith and Blydenburgh families that includes a mill, a miller's house and a farm cottage. The complex, which is listed on the National Register of Historic Places, illustrates the interconnection between farming, grain production and milling activities.

As areas of Long Island became more densely populated, resourceful bakers responded with new services and found that they were feeding an insatiable public appetite for breads and baked goods. German immigrant William Entenmann opened a bakery in Brooklyn in 1898 and established a home delivery service for his freshly baked breads and cakes, using a horse-drawn wagon. When the health of Entenmann's son forced the family to move to Bay Shore, Long Island, he relocated his business and established thirty home delivery routes. By the 1950s, the Entenmann family had abandoned home delivery and bread production. The company focused on cakes and pastries and became a national brand distributed in forty-eight states; it was acquired by a parent company, Bimbo Bakeries USA, in 2002. By 2014, the iconic Entenmann's Bakery in Bay Shore was forced to close, a victim of rising taxes and labor costs. It had become such a fixture on Long Island that Bay Shore's Fifth Avenue was known as "Entenmann's Way." The bakery had operated there in some form since 1905.

For many decades during the twentieth century, Long Island City in Queens was a hub for commercial bakeries servicing the populace of Manhattan, Long Island and the tri-state region. Fink Baking Corporation and the Silvercup Bakery were among the top names, with Silvercup mass-producing a popular soft, white sandwich loaf. Long Island City was the breadbasket of the metropolitan region. One could inhale the intoxicating aroma of freshly baking bread from Manhattan to Queens. Both Fink Baking and Silvercup Bakery closed after years of operations, and the former Silvercup Bakery is now home to a film and television production studio.

Today, corner bakeries and commercially produced breads are plentiful on Long Island. Most packaged breads are manufactured out of state, where businesses take advantage of lower production costs. But as public tastes move toward bread made with simple ingredients and no artificial additives, there is a distinctive shift toward handmade, artisan breads. New bakers and entrepreneurs who embrace classic European bread techniques are emerging. Some sell their small-batch breads through local farmers' markets or health food stores. Others use the latest technology to produce a higher volume of breads with appealing artisan characteristics and sell wholesale to high-end restaurants. The integrity of the baker, the quality of the ingredients and the heartiness of the bread are all critical elements in a resurgence of bread, carefully tended and made the old-fashioned way.

BLUE DUCK BAKERY CAFÉ

In a world of presliced supermarket breads and mom and pop bakeries, Keith Kouris has engendered attention and appreciation from Montauk to Manhattan for artisan, old-world breads and classic pastries. Kouris co-founded Blue Duck Bakery Café with his wife, Nancy, in 1999 and set up their first shop in Southampton. Kouris said that he was hooked on baking the first time he set foot in a professional kitchen and inhaled the aroma of bread baking in the oven. As a one-time owner of a bread delivery route and a successful bakery manager for a large supermarket chain, Kouris was experienced with the state of mass-produced bread on Long Island, but he had a different vision.

Since opening, Blue Duck Bakery has expanded to four different retail locations on the North and South Forks that include stores in Southampton, Greenport and Riverhead. The Southold location contains a large production facility connected to the storefront that can produce up to thirty varieties of European-style bread.

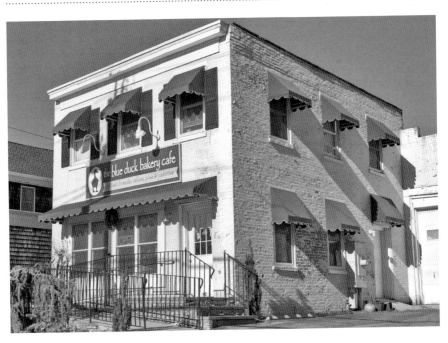

Exterior of Blue Duck Bakery Café, Southold. *Photo by Jacob Skoglund.*

From the beginning, the retail cafés—decorated with images of the bakery's azure web-footed mascot—were an important dimension of the business. "I think it's so important that the community know who you are and trust who you are," explained Kouris.

Enter one of the Blue Duck Bakery's charming storefront cafés—adorned with splashes of French blue—and you encounter rustic baskets stuffed with picture-perfect French baguettes and chewy loaves and boules leavened by natural fermentation. There's a wide selection for all types of artisan bread devotees, including whole grain, sourdough, French batards, German rye, sauerkraut rye and an indulgent chocolate bread that pairs with cheese or makes for a heavenly dessert. Kouris said that his breads evoke a distinctive sense of place that can only be found on the East End of Long Island. "The Long Island Sound, the ocean, the farms and the vineyards all generate wild yeast that help the bread to rise."

The bakery case delights the senses with an eye-popping array of fancy celebration cakes, cupcakes, pies, cheesecake, cannoli, éclairs and Napoleons. Lunchtime visitors can chose from sandwiches, soups and quiches.

The Southold bakery hums with activity as staff members knead, shape and score a staggering selection of breads for baking. Blue Duck Bakery

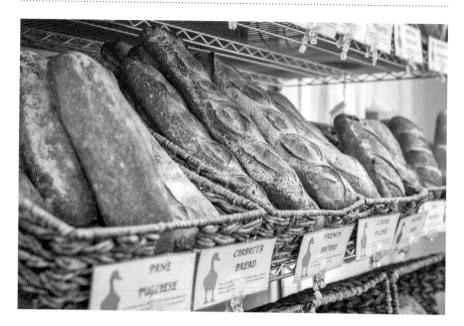

Artisan baguettes at Blue Duck Bakery Café. *Photo by Jacob Skoglund.*

manages a significant wholesale business that supplies to restaurants, cafés, grocery stores and other retail outlets in New York City, Long Island and New Jersey. It is a large operation, and the right equipment helps to ensure a high yield of product with the desired artisan quality. "Technology has been slightly ahead of the artisan baker," said Kouris as he surveyed the sophisticated baking apparatus within the production facility.

Kouris is a friendly, down-to-earth man who learned baking from the ground up, and he is well versed in the complexities of production and distribution. "I had the entrepreneur bug in me," he said. After years of working the bread delivery route and owning a family deli, Kouris tried out for a job in the bakery department of a prominent local supermarket chain. He had no hands-on baking experience. "I was never so intimidated in my life. I knew I wasn't a baker, but they hired me anyway. I was very lucky."

At the time, supermarket bakeries were just starting to become fixtures in stores, and the supermarket chain was willing to experiment with new styles of bread. Kouris learned from several experienced bakers on staff and began building his skills. "They had a lot of knowledge to impart," he said. "I learned from Italian, Jewish and German bakers—all kinds of guys."

Soon, Kouris was put in charge of one of the store bakeries and began helping the chain open more bakeries throughout Long Island. He

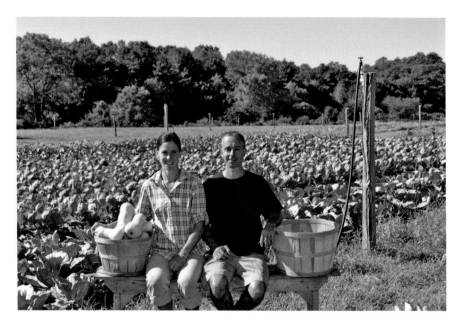

Caroline Fanning and Dan Holmes are head growers at Restoration Farm in Old Bethpage. *Courtesy Adrian Fanning.*

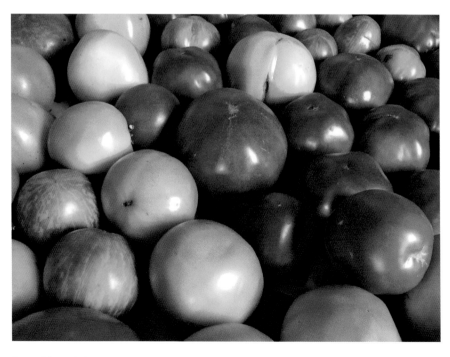

Long Island heirloom tomatoes offer a colorful palette of flavor each summer. *Photo by T.W. Barritt.*

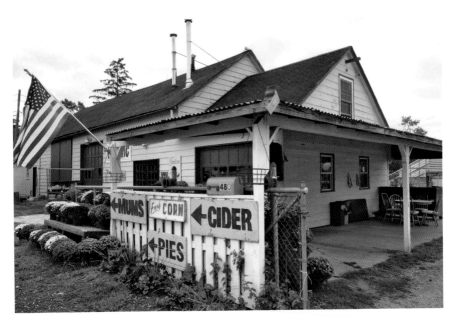

Crossroads Farm at Grossmann's operates on the site of an original family farm in Malverne. *Photo by T.W. Barritt.*

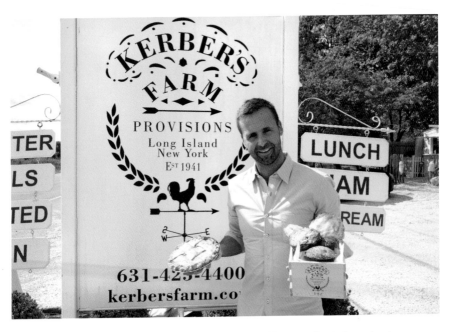

Huntington native Nick Voulgaris III restored Kerber's Farm, saving it from developers. *Photo by T.W. Barritt.*

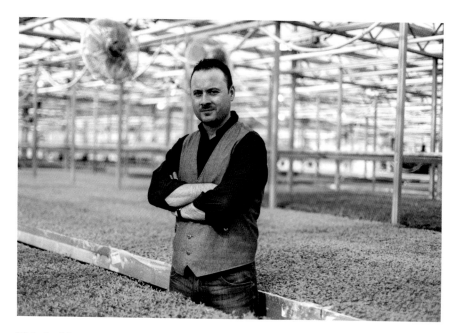

Nicholas Mazard heads Koppert Cress, a micro-greens company that cultivates inspiration for chefs. *Photo by Jacob Skoglund.*

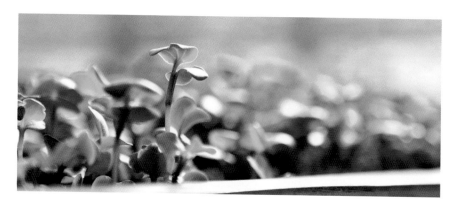

The seeds for Koppert Cress micro-greens are sourced from all over the world. *Photo by Jacob Skoglund.*

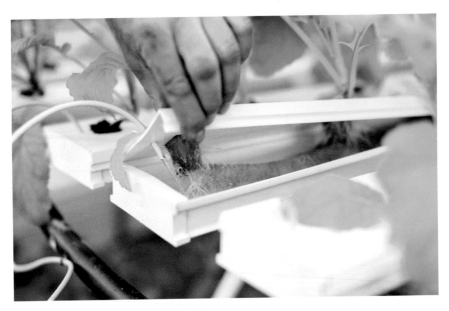

Roots of hydroponic greens at Thera Farms are nourished using nutrient-rich water. *Photo by Jacob Skoglund.*

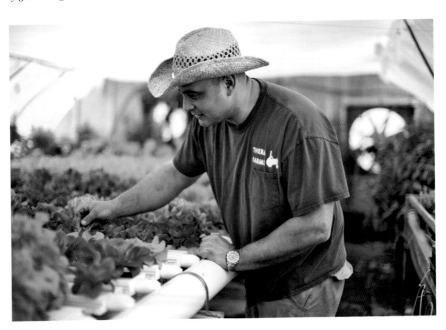

Teddy Bolkas of Ronkonkoma grows hydroponic lettuce year-round at Thera Farms. *Photo by Jacob Skoglund.*

Opposite, top: The catch of the day at Freeport's Nautical Mile. *Photo by Jacob Skoglund.*

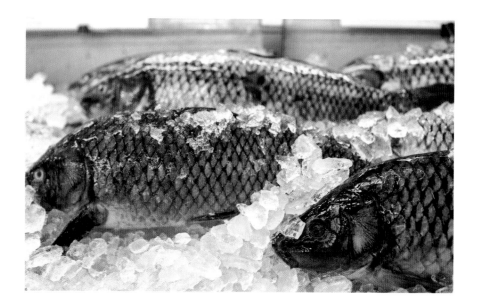

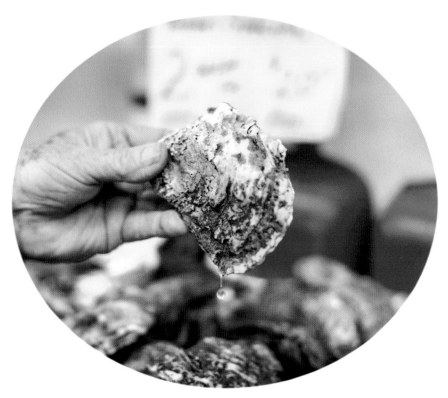

Local oysters are integral to Long Island's historic maritime food culture. *Photo by Jacob Skoglund.*

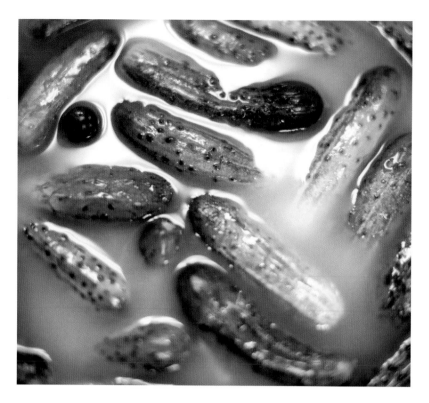

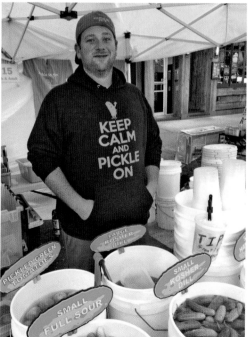

Above: Horman's Best Pickles are a fixture at Long Island farmers' markets. *Photo by Jacob Skoglund.*

Left: Pete Starr is founder of Pickle Me Pete. *Photo by T.W. Barritt.*

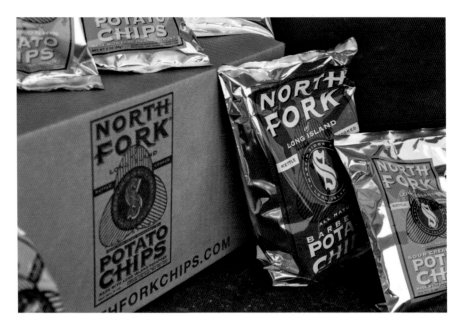

North Fork Potato Chips are made from the iconic Long Island potato. *Photo by Jacob Skoglund.*

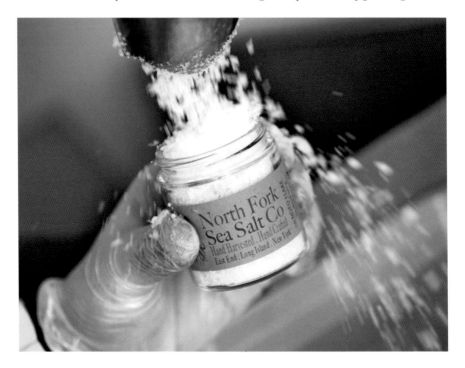

North Fork Sea Salt Company sources sea salt from the waters surrounding Long Island. *Courtesy Randee Daddona.*

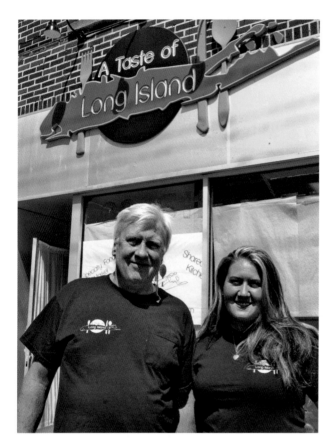

Left: Jim Thompson and Courtney Citko created A Taste of Long Island to market products made by local food entrepreneurs. *Photo by T.W. Barritt.*

Below: The Big Cheese sells Long Island and New York State cheeses at local farmers' markets. *Photo by Jacob Skoglund.*

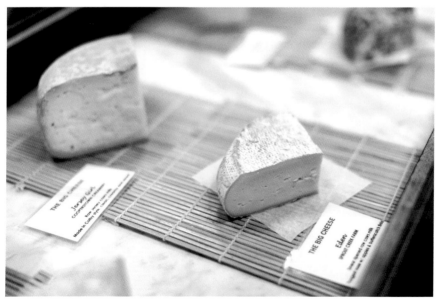

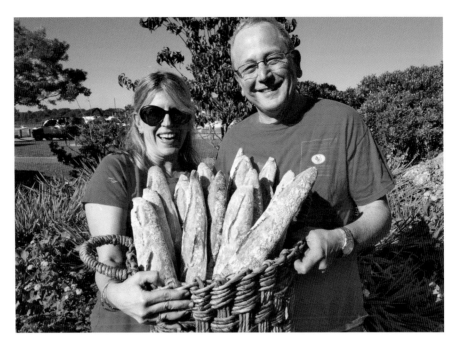

Sherri and Bob Biancavilla of Duck Island Bread Company in Huntington. *Photo by T.W. Barritt.*

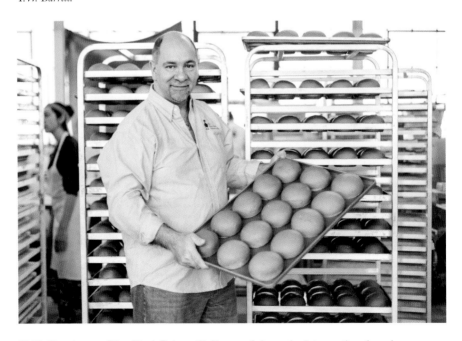

Keith Kouris owns Blue Duck Bakery Café, one of the nation's top artisan bread companies. *Photo by Jacob Skoglund.*

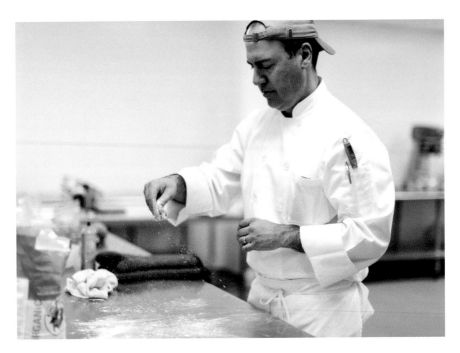

David Shalam founded Heritage Bakers to offer Long Islanders healthy baked goods. *Photo by Jacob Skoglund.*

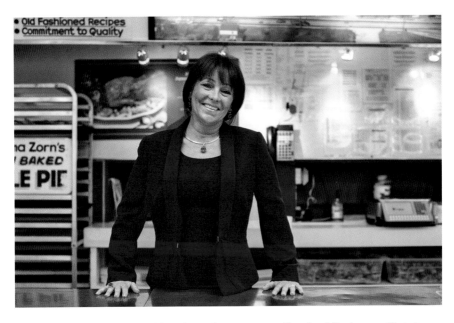

Merrill Zorn is CEO of the historic poultry company Zorn's of Bethpage. *Photo by Jacob Skoglund.*

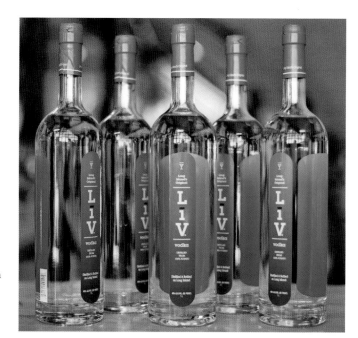

LiV Vodka, distilled by Long Island Spirits, is hand-crafted from locally grown Long Island potatoes. *Photo by Jacob Skoglund.*

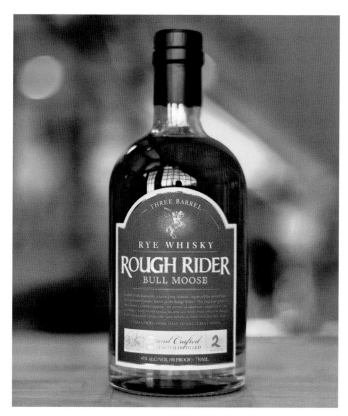

Rough Rider Bourbon made by Long Island Spirits in Baiting Hollow. *Photo by Jacob Skoglund.*

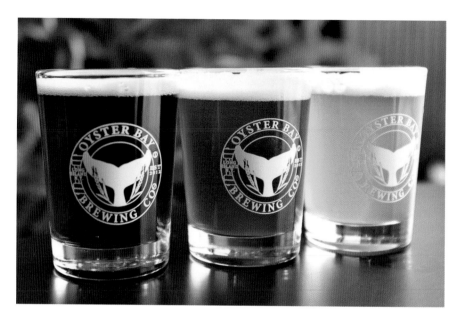

Three styles of craft beer from the Oyster Bay Brewing Company. *Photo by John Barritt.*

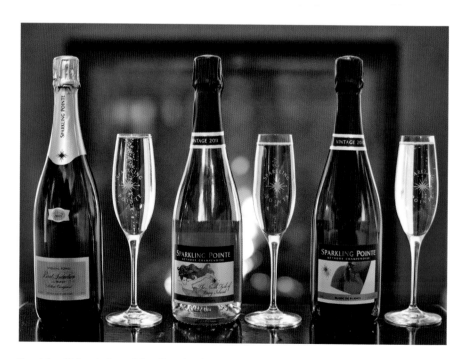

Sparkling Pointe is Long Island's only winery devoted exclusively to Méthode Champenoise–style wine. *Photo by Jacob Skoglund.*

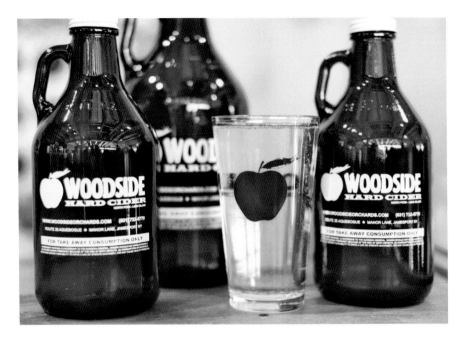

Woodside Orchards of Aquebogue is home to Long Island's first hard cidery. *Photo by Jacob Skoglund.*

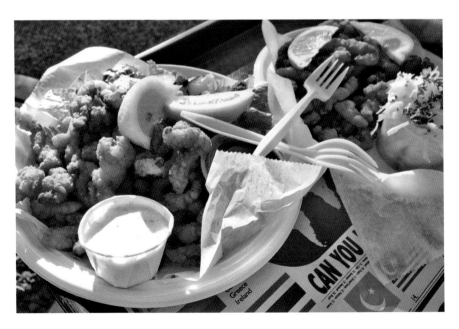

The fried clams at the Shack in Centerport are a summertime favorite. *Photo by T.W. Barritt.*

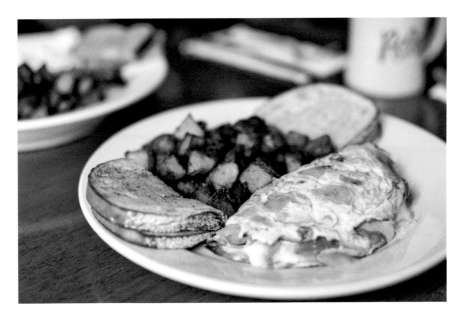

The restaurant Relish in Kings Park uses eggs sourced from nearby Raleigh's Poultry Farm. *Photo by Jacob Skoglund.*

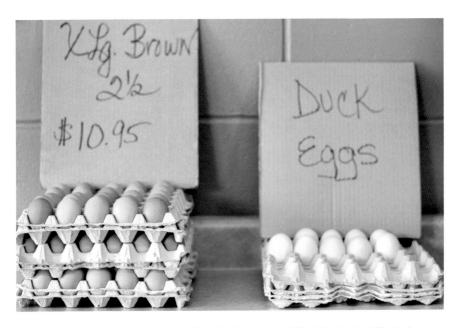

Raleigh's Poultry Farm has operated in Kings Park since the 1960s. *Photo by Jacob Skoglund.*

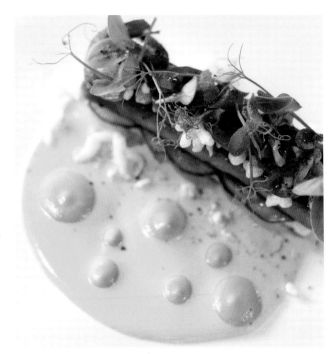

The pressed pork belly chulo, with toasted brioche, pickled red onion and cucumber and house mustard, served at Roots Bistro Gourmand in West Islip. *Photo by Jacob Skoglund.*

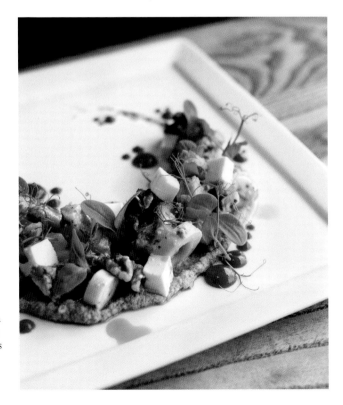

Octopus with artichoke heart, walnut, heart of palm and charred eggplant puree, served at Roots Bistro Gourmand in West Islip. *Photo by Jacob Skoglund.*

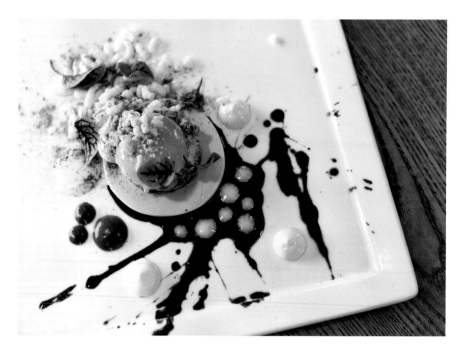

Steak tartare with slow-cooked egg yolk, aged Gouda panna cotta and squid ink served at Roots Bistro Gourmand in West Islip. *Photo by Jacob Skoglund.*

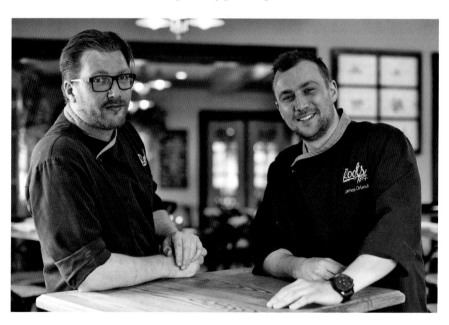

Philippe Corbet and James Orlandi are chefs and co-owners of Roots Bistro Gourmand. *Photo by Jacob Skoglund.*

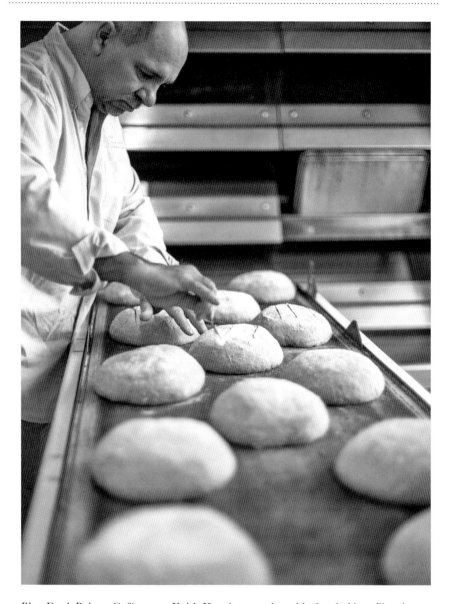

Blue Duck Bakery Café owner Keith Kouris scores bread before baking. *Photo by Jacob Skoglund.*

continually experimented with different styles of bread and took classes on artisan bread baking. Most important, he was delivering impressive business results. "I was giving them the highest-grossing department numbers out of all the bakeries," said Kouris. But as the store changed its approach to the bakery business, Kouris decided that the time was right to focus his efforts on his own artisan breads and pastries.

Blue Duck Bakery mirrors Kouris's life experiences. He is the classic neighborhood baker but has also leveraged the best of a large commercial operation and distribution network to offer outstanding artisan baked goods to the broader community beyond Long Island. Blue Duck Bakery has been honored for the quality of its breads and pastries. *Saveur* magazine named Blue Duck Bakery one of the top twenty artisan bakeries in America in 2012, and in 2015, it was named one of the top ten artisan bakeries in North America by *Dessert Professional* magazine.

Blue Duck Bakery Café
30 Hampton Road
Southampton, NY, 11968
631-204-1701

130 Front Street
Greenport, NY, 11944
631-333-2060

309 East Main Street
Riverhead, NY, 11901
631-591-2710

56275 Main Road
Southold, NY, 11971
631-629-4123
blueduckbakerycafe.com

DUCK ISLAND BREAD COMPANY

Time, touch, flavor and a love of community are all baked into the European-style artisan breads and pastries that Robert Biancavilla has sold at the Northport Farmers' Market for several years. With Duck Island Bread Company, founder and head baker Biancavilla has revived the romantic notion of the hometown baker who hand-crafts all his goods from scratch and knows his patrons by name. His open-air booth is filled with woven baskets overflowing with the perfect pastries, cinnamon buns, baguettes, brioche and fougasse that one might expect to find in a classic Parisian bake shop. The distinctive Duck Island Bread Company orange signage attracts browsers at the waterfront market who crave a buttery croissant and a cup of coffee to start their day or a loaf of rustic bread to nourish their weekend.

Amid the frantic pace of suburban life, Duck Island Bread Company promises that no bread is baked before its time. Biancavilla feeds several different types of starter dough, which he has nurtured for years. Each batch of dough develops a deep, distinctive flavor through hours of fermentation. He shapes each loaf and pastry item by hand. "I think people appreciate when someone makes something from scratch," said Biancavilla.

Equally enticing is the story behind the bread. Biancavilla's day job is as deputy bureau chief, Homicide Bureau, for the Suffolk County District Attorney's Office. He spends his weekdays prosecuting accused murderers, and on Friday evenings—when his typical workweek concludes—he drives to a commercial bakery and embraces his second vocation. There, Biancavilla begins to work with the dough that has been fermenting during the week. He will stay up all night, shaping, rolling, proofing and baking pastries and loaves that are delivered to the farmers' market early on Saturday morning. Then he works the booth with his wife, Sherri, and other family members, greeting neighbors and sharing tantalizing tidbits about the different breads. His head might finally hit the pillow by Saturday afternoon.

A native of East Williston, Biancavilla earned money baking bagels during high school and college. Years later, as he considered a plan for retirement, he investigated classes on artisan bread baking and trained at the French Culinary Institute in New York and King Arthur Flour in Vermont. He founded Duck Island Bread Company in 2011.

Duck Island Bread Company uses a French-made hearth oven. Loaves are baked on a stone deck, and a burst of steam injected from the oven helps ensure a classic, crisp crust. Biancavilla usually offers patrons a choice of more than half a dozen types of bread and more than a dozen different pastries. His volume has doubled year over year, and he expresses appreciation for the loyalty of his customers. Biancavilla has embraced social media, sharing bread photos and techniques with fellow bakers on Twitter and Instagram. He often experiments with recipes and adds new varieties to his menu, but he never seems to lose his sense of wonder over a simple, freshly baked artisan baguette. "It's worth staying up all night to pull something like that out of the oven," he said.

Newsday food writer Erica Marcus recognized Duck Island Bread Company for Best Bread of 2014. In the spring of 2015, Biancavilla realized a longtime dream, opening his first retail shop in the town of Huntington.

Duck Island Bread Company
201C East Main Street
Huntington, NY, 11743
631-223-2799
duckislandbreadcompany.com

HERITAGE BAKERS

Like many suburban parents, David and Deborah Shalam were becoming increasingly concerned about the quality of the food their family was consuming. The Sea Cliff couple questioned the healthfulness of mass-produced, processed foods. Surrounded by national fast-food chains and pizza joints, they wondered if they could come up with something healthier on their own to feed their three children. "We realized we had to eat better, so we changed our diets," said David.

With his consumer electronics job at a crossroads, he took it upon himself to create a new approach for his family and an alternate business and career path for himself. "I'd always been kind of an amateur baker," he explained. "I always made the popovers for Thanksgiving." He even recalled setting up a street-side bake stand to earn money when he was eight years old. So, he enrolled in an intensive six-month baking course at the French Culinary Institute in New York City in search of a career transition. If mass-produced bread was seen as progress, David had other ideas. "So many people are concerned about their food, but no one ever questions the bread," he said. "Most of modern wheat these days is full of garbage. They've hybridized the wheat for greater yields. It looks like wheat and tastes like wheat, but our bodies break it down like sugar."

While researching ingredients for a potential baking business, the Shalams discovered a healthier option in heirloom grains that were cultivated for several centuries before industrialization changed the nature of farming and bread baking in the United States. Working through the Calverton Business Incubator Kitchen, David founded the company Heritage Bakers in 2014, offering artisanal breads and an eclectic selection

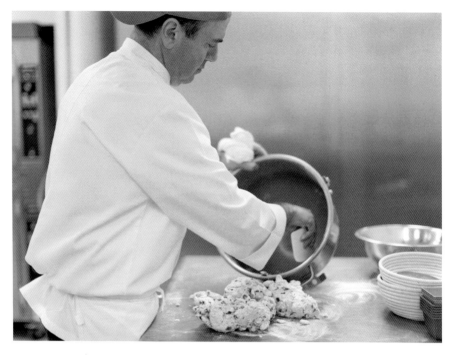

David Shalam of Heritage Bakers preparing scones. *Photo by Jacob Skoglund.*

of popovers, cookies and scones made with organic heirloom whole wheat flour. Heritage Bakers sells baked goods online and at farmers' markets throughout Long Island. Their first retail outlet was Rising Tide Natural Market in Glen Cove, a pioneering health food store that first opened in 1976 and caters to a health-minded consumer.

"We're trying to create a new tradition," David explained. "We're trying to take the old quality and the old ways and reintroduce them."

The main ingredient in their breads and baked goods is Red Fife Whole Wheat flour, a hearty grain used in the nineteenth century. Red Fife grain is grown in western Canada and milled fresh on demand at a facility in North Carolina. David said that the Red Fife flour adds a nuttiness that you don't taste in other breads. "The flavors are just tremendous. It stays with you, it's heartier and it's nice to know that you're using something that was grown part and parcel to the way it was and with a minimal amount of processing."

As a baker, he appreciates that Red Fife pairs nicely with anything from chocolate chips to berries. "With this flour, you can almost marry it to anything and you get such a positive result."

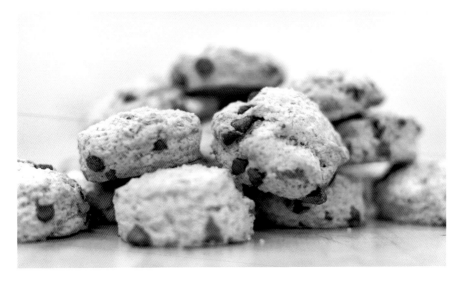

Scones from Heritage Bakers are baked with flour made from heirloom grain. *Photo by Jacob Skoglund.*

Heritage Bakers is a family enterprise. David is head baker, his wife handles packaging and his children often help out at farmers' markets. He likes using the farmers' market to reach customers in multiple communities. "It's a great way to connect with people, and for people who really want to know the story, you can talk it through and make some nice connections." He enjoys the instant feedback from customers and uses the opportunity to share the story of heirloom grains. "I want to be customer facing," he said. "I love talking to people, and I love educating them."

An advocate for healthful eating, David believes that there is opportunity for small businesses that want to make a statement with their work. "There is room for people like myself who are going to do it the real way. It might cost more money, it might take more effort, but I think it produces such a better-quality product."

Heritage Bakers
516-456-0216
heritagebakers.com

Chapter 8
Birds of a Feather

For the casual motorist traversing Route 24 in Flanders, the sight of a colossal white duck with a bright yellow beak and piercing eyes perched at the side of the road can be somewhat arresting. Many travelers will abruptly stop the car, jump out for a quick snapshot and then continue their journey. To them, the enormous aquatic invader is outrageous roadside art or yet another quirky Long Island curiosity.

Built in 1931 to house a store where Riverhead duck farmer Martin Maurer sold locally raised duck products, the Big Duck stands twenty feet tall and thirty feet wide. Conceived by a team of Broadway set designers, the duck was constructed of a wooden frame reinforced with concrete. Two taillights, salvaged from a Model T Ford, gave the duck its glowing red eyes, visible to drivers at night. Over the course of decades, the Big Duck faced demolition and threats from developers yet still managed to survive thanks to a vocal group of supporters. The building was donated to Suffolk County in 1987 and has been relocated three times. It is now listed on the National Register of Historic Places and is home to an information center and a gift shop for duck memorabilia. Curators established a small museum on the property devoted to the history of duck farming on Long Island.

The Big Duck of Long Island is more than just a Disneyesque attraction or a historic oddity. It is a symbol of one of Long Island's enduring products of origin. The unpredictable and sometimes improbable "journey" of the Big Duck seems to parallel the path of duck farming and poultry production on Long Island.

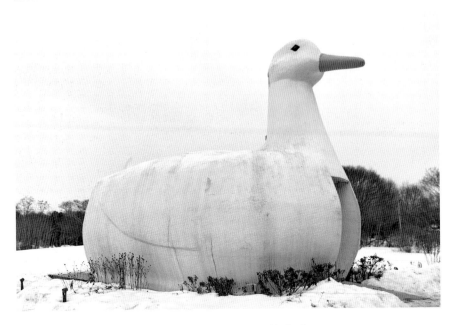

The Big Duck of Long Island, Flanders. *Photo by Jacob Skoglund.*

Poultry production on Long Island has its origins in family farming. An individual family might keep several backyard chickens to ensure a steady supply of eggs. When hens were no longer productive, they were slaughtered for meat. Immigrants trained in butchery and entrepreneurial farmers took note that the wide-open spaces and availability of fresh water on Long Island were favorable to raising larger flocks. They expanded family businesses and created a demand for a more plentiful supply of quality eggs and poultry. Some became avid marketers, presenting Long Island duck and poultry as products with a touch of cachet. As operations increased, so did the cost of production and the impact on the environment.

Once plentiful land became more valuable to developers, younger family members sought new professions. Many families sold their land and got out of the business. The cost of new environmental regulations also put greater stress on profits. Poultry production during the twentieth century on Long Island somewhat mimics a typical bell curve, with a steep increase and then a gradual decline. In the first decades of the twenty-first century, it is a niche business with a handful of enduring family farms and specialty operations. In some cases, we are even seeing a return to families who keep free-range, backyard hens as a response to public dismay over factory farming practices by large corporations.

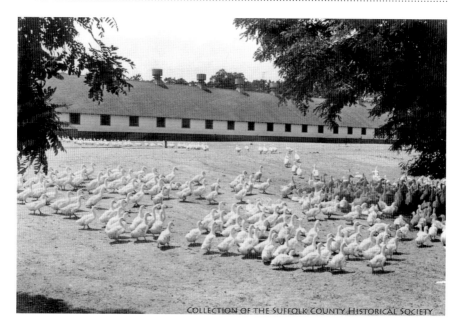

Talmage Duck Farm. Undated. *Copyright © Collection of the Suffolk County Historical Society.*

A fading, antique Kodachrome postcard on file at the Suffolk County Historical Society proclaims, "Roast Long Island Duckling is fit for a king." Indeed, in its heyday during the mid-twentieth century, Long Island was the source of origin for nearly two-thirds of the duck eaten in the United States. Like the succulent flesh of the bird itself, the legacy of duck production lends itself to some juicy stories. The breed commonly known as Long Island duckling is actually Pekin duck from China. Various duck producers and cookbook authors like to share the story of James E. Palmer of Connecticut, who reportedly brought the first Pekin ducks to the United States, arriving in New York City in 1873.

Plump and with abundant flesh, the Pekin duck matured in only ten to twelve weeks and was quickly seen as a lucrative option for farmers looking to build their business. Smaller duck farms operating on the eastern end of Long Island quickly turned to the Pekin duck as their bird of choice, as it was well suited to commercial farming. Early farms raised ducks on "dry" ranches, but farmers later realized that allowing ducks access to fresh water at streams and creeks was more cost-effective.

Long Island entrepreneurs seized the opportunity, and duck farming became a boom business from Nassau County to the East End. The Atlantic Duck Farm in Speonk, owned by Warren W. Hallock, began operation around 1858 and by 1938 was the largest duck farm in the world, producing 260,000 ducks. The tiny town of Eastport had the highest concentration of duck farms in the region until the 1970s and was referred to as the "Duck Capital of the World."

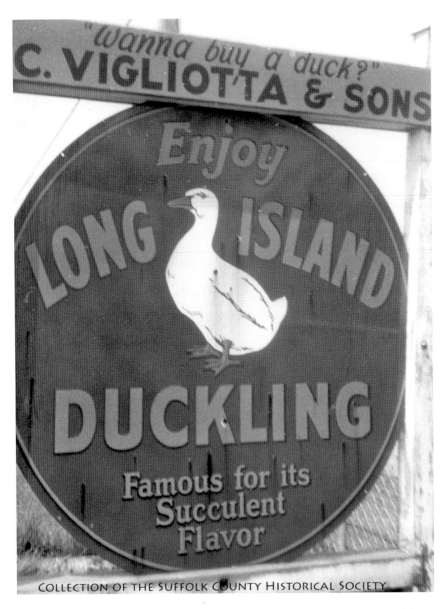

Long Island duck farming at C. Vigliotta & Sons. Undated. *Copyright © Collection of the Suffolk County Historical Society.*

As duck production rapidly expanded, the Long Island duckling gained fame. The growing railroad system transported product to New York restaurants and beyond, supplying hungry diners across the nation. A restaurant named John Duck's, operating first in Eastport and then in Southampton, was popular with local celebrities and renowned for its recipe for roast Long Island duckling with Bing cherry sauce for nearly a century. When producers found themselves with a surplus of ducks in 1960, more than forty farmers banded together, formed the Long Island Duck Farmers Cooperative and implemented a nationwide marketing campaign extolling the virtue of Long Island duck. Production hit its peak in the early 1960s at 7.5 million ducks annually.

While perhaps not the marvel of marketing that was Long Island duckling, chicken and turkey prospered on Long Island as well. Beginning in the 1940s, German immigrant Peter Zorn and his family operated eight poultry farms in various Long Island towns, producing turkey and chicken to support both successful wholesale and retail operations. Miloski's Poultry Farm was established in 1946 in Calverton. Makinajian Poultry Farm opened in Huntington in 1948. All continue to do business today, although only Miloski's Poultry Farm still raises free-range turkeys on the premises, while the others have outsourced production of live birds. New poultry models are emerging. Browder's Birds, a small operation that raises certified organic chicken and eggs in Mattituck, is giving new meaning to the old phrase "a chicken in every pot." Browder's offers a twenty-week chicken share to members who can pick up an organic, pasture-raised chicken each Saturday.

Several factors forced the decline of Long Island's duck industry. Summer visitors to the East End complained about the odor and waste emitted from the farms. In fact, severe pollution of freshwater streams caused by duck farms prompted regulators to impose strict environmental regulations and pollution control measures that many farmers found too costly. As property taxes and operating costs increased, some farmers moved out of state, while others shut down. Some sold their property to land developers. By 2009, there were only three remaining duck farms responsible for annual production of more than 2 million ducks. In 2011, the Jurgielewicz Duck Farm in Moriches closed amid environmental concerns. Chester Massey & Sons Duck Farm in Eastport closed at the end of 2014, citing the costs of strict environmental regulations. Only Crescent Duck Farm in Aquebogue remains in operation.

CRESCENT DUCK FARM

The Corwin family—owner of Long Island's only surviving duck farm—is descended from one of the first English families who settled on the East End of Long Island. Perhaps it is that pioneering spirit that has helped Crescent Duck Farm in Aquebogue to evolve with the times and prosper while other Long Island duck farmers were forced to fold. Crescent Duck Farm produces 1 million ducks annually and is single-handedly keeping luscious, Long Island duckling on the menu at fine restaurants and in markets throughout the region.

In 1640, Matthias Corwin was part of a group that traveled to Long Island seeking religious freedom. Corwin settled in Southold and acquired land on the North Fork now known as Aquebogue. Corwin's descendants farmed the land and worked as carpenters for generations. By the start of the twentieth century, Henry Corwin, a carpenter, wondered how he might make better use of a sandy patch of land near a creek on the family homestead. In 1908, Henry purchased thirty breeding ducks. The sandy area and stream were the perfect terrain for ducks to prosper. One year later, Henry turned to duck farming full time. Soon, he was raising four thousand ducks annually. Over the next century, Crescent Duck Farm would grow and evolve as the family responded to changes in the marketplace and the regulatory environment.

Douglas Corwin is a fourth-generation farmer in the family business and the president of Crescent Duck Farm. Today, the farm has outlived the competition, which succumbed to challenging economics and the high cost of stringent environmental regulations.

Crescent Duck Farm now spans more than 140 acres and maintains the highest standard for modern duck farming. Corwin, who studied agricultural economics at Cornell University, has developed progressive feeding regimens and breeding programs that result in a more succulent, meatier bird. He also invests heavily in waste treatment and environmental protection. Unlike the past, ducks are now raised indoors, and there is a multimillion-dollar state-of-the-art sewage treatment facility on the farm. Family members provide daily care to the flocks. Corwin's two sons have joined the business and are part of the multigenerational effort to preserve and protect Long Island's duck farming legacy.

Crescent Duck Farm
PO Box 500
Aquebogue, NY, 11931
crescentduck.com

Makinajian Poultry Farm

A framed watercolor painting hangs over the counter at Makinajian Poultry Farm in Huntington. It depicts a whimsical, animated character running at an exaggerated speed and clutching a large white egg. Beneath him is the motto, "We Sell the Best to You!"

Michael "Mick" Makinajian's grandfather Joseph painted the picture and had at one time intended the character and slogan to serve as the mission and logo for the Makinajian Poultry Farm, which he established in 1948. Today, Michael and his two sisters are caretakers of Joseph's vision.

The Saturday morning traffic can be daunting on Route 25, where auto dealers, nail salons, clothing stores, doughnut shops and even a gentlemen's club proliferate. Heading east on Elmont Road, the scene shifts quickly to large, almost monstrous suburban homes, an athletic field, a smattering of churches and a school. Approaching Makinajian's is like being transported to an earlier era. A fenced barnyard is populated with sheep, ducks and geese. Just beyond the gravel parking lot, there is a tidy, red-shingled store, a barn and a labyrinth of chicken coops. In the shop, the heady aroma of roasted chicken can provoke an appetite well before lunch. The refrigerator case is stocked with plump, fresh chicken, and there is a variety of brown and white eggs for sale, as well as some impressively sized goose eggs. There is a steady stream of customers cradling market baskets and inspecting produce, specialty salads and freshly baked breads and pies.

When Michael's grandfather Joseph—an immigrant from Armenia—purchased the Huntington property and moved his family from Queens in 1948, he got started with three hundred chickens. The land had most likely been a farm, and the adjacent road was named for the Cuba family who owned the land. "My grandfather was always a farmer and a beekeeper," said Michael. "He took a beekeeping course at Cornell by mail and had a victory garden in the city. He would sell eggs out of the basement of the house, and we grew hay in the back."

Joseph was the quintessential Long Islander and a pioneering commuter. He held a job as a projectionist at a movie theater in New York City and traveled by train to Manhattan each day. Farming, however, was his avocation and always a part of his daily routine. "He took care of the chickens in the morning," explained Michael. "Then he would take the train to the city and sell chickens and eggs at the markets."

Joseph passed away in the late 1950s, at which point Michael's father, Edward, took over the family business. "He taught everything to my father, and

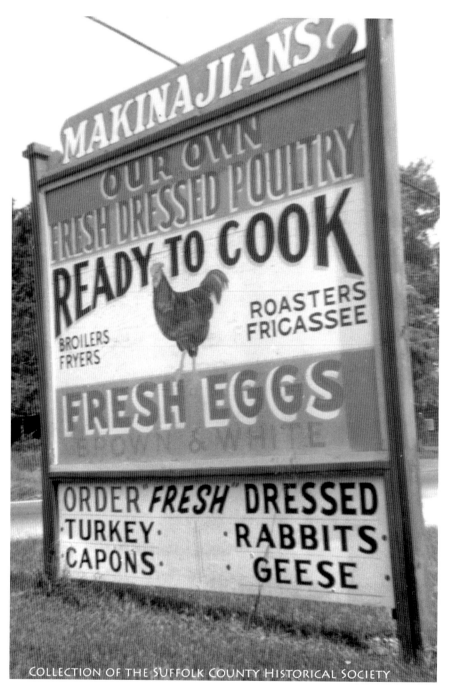

Makinajian's poultry sign. Undated. *Copyright © Collection of the Suffolk County Historical Society.*

my father was the only one who wanted to run the farm out of the three kids. So when my grandfather died, my father had to make a go of the farm."

Edward was clearly driven to make the business succeed. "He fixed up the barns, and he started delivering eggs and chickens door to door," said Michael.

One wall of the store offers a pictorial history of the Makinajian family business. A yellowed clipping from a 1964 edition of a Suffolk County agricultural publication shows Michael's father, Edward, smiling behind the counter of his new retail store, with cartons of eggs stacked high in front of him. According to the article, the day after Edward erected his new sign on Cuba Hill Road, his sales of poultry meat more than doubled. "In 1964, my father made this garage and workshop into a little store. He wanted to have a retail place so he didn't have to go and deliver anymore. He realized that retail was the way to go, and that was the way we were going to continue the farm."

A 1972 clipping from *Newsday* portrays Edward as a fountainhead of egg expertise. His reputation was well deserved. Edward had begun packing eggs when he was ten years old. Even in 1972, Edward was discussing the nutritional benefits of white versus brown eggs, a debate that continues to this day. His determination led to significant expansion of the business.

"At one point, we had ten thousand laying hens on this farm, and we were Long Island's largest egg producer," said Michael. "My father started a route and would deliver to country clubs and delis and restaurants. In the 1970s, I'd get in the van with my father, and we'd go do deliveries. It was a lot of fun, but I didn't realize how much pressure my father was under to make ends meet and keep the farm."

Now in his mid-forties, Michael said that the family has continued to reinvent the farm. Once the egg market was regulated, prices dropped due to competition from poultry farms in the South. His father looked to diversify and realized that a six-acre farm with a generous supply of chicken manure presented an opportunity. The family began raising produce, and the farm was certified organic in 1993. "Because we never used chemicals, it was easy for us to get certified organic," noted Michael. "We started growing berries and vegetables in the back and selling them in the store."

Makinajian's remains a family operation to this day. While poultry production has declined from the farm's heyday, the chicken coops are full; they still sell fresh-killed poultry, rotisserie chicken and fresh eggs and supplement their homegrown produce with items from other organic farms. Makinajian's also sells fresh-cut flowers in the summer. Michael's sister Victoria prepares all the baked goods sold at the store, and his sister Tina works the counter. Michael believes that their focus on organic produce is a big attraction for his loyal clientele, but it goes far beyond that.

"They're buying us—they're buying the Makinajian family. They trust us, and they know that we only sell the best. That's our motto—the best eggs, the best poultry, the best berries, the best vegetables."

Makinajian Poultry Farm & Country Store
276 Cuba Hill Road
Huntington, NY, 11743
631-368-9320

ZORN'S OF BETHPAGE

Merrill Zorn sits in the office of Zorn's of Bethpage recalling how her family started the company seventy-five years ago. She is the de facto family historian and has been contacting elderly relatives to try and capture as many of their memories as possible. The past influences so much of what happens at Zorn's. As it says on the Zorn's delivery truck, there's "a little bit of history in every bite."

The office interior of the venerable poultry and catering retail store is covered in a style of wood paneling that was popular in the 1970s. Once surrounded by farmland, the Zorn's store is now enclosed by a busy hospital, service stations and banks. The footprint of the enterprise has evolved and changed since Merrill's grandfather Peter Zorn first started his new retail venture in the early 1940s, offering "oven ready" turkeys to suburban households.

"This is the original store right here," said Merrill, referring to her office. "My grandfather took a sawhorse, and my grandmother put a piece of plywood on it and an oilcloth and this is where they started." The idea was revolutionary. Peter Zorn transformed the turkey from a holiday staple to a year-round delicacy.

Merrill is a gregarious woman in her early fifties. She is president and CEO of Zorn's of Bethpage, but she's been working at the establishment most of her life. "We were old school, so if I wanted a bicycle, I would have to work for it," she explained. "I probably started working here when I was about seven years old. I would make potpie tops, and I remember mixing the mincemeat and apples for the pies. I was the only kid out of the family that worked in every department."

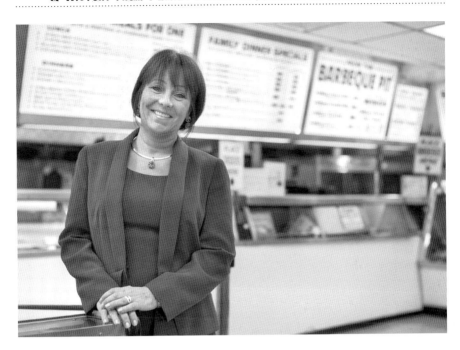

Merrill Zorn is CEO at Zorn's of Bethpage and family historian for the enduring poultry business. *Photo by Jacob Skoglund.*

Peter Zorn's story began long before he took a gamble and opened the Bethpage store in 1940. At one time, the Zorn's family business included a retail store and numerous poultry farms. Born in Bruschsal, Germany, in 1907, Peter Zorn immigrated to the United States in 1925, shortly after his sister had made the journey. A butcher by trade, he worked on a farm in Montgomery, New York, and later in Poughkeepsie. Eventually, he moved to New York City and worked as a butcher for eight years. He met his future wife, Gesine, at a social event in Queens, and they were married in 1929.

The Northeast climate and soil were favorable for raising eggs and poultry, and Zorn was a hard worker and shrewd businessman who understood how to market meats and poultry. He established a poultry business in Flushing, New York, under his own name but had an eye on expansion. Land surrounding New York City was plentiful, and within several years, Peter Zorn, his father and four siblings were operating eight poultry farms located in Bethpage, Central Islip, Bohemia, Hauppauge (two locations), Glenwood Landing, Brentwood and Smithtown. A ninth farm was established in Mullica Hill, New Jersey.

In 1940, Zorn established the Bethpage location, which included a twenty-three-thousand-egg-capacity turkey incubator with all the necessary modern equipment. He purchased used buildings from the World's Fair to use as poultry houses and offices. Those structures still stand today on both sides of the main building.

At the time, all of the Zorn family farms raised chickens and sold them wholesale to vendors in the New York City area. Turkeys were sold only at Christmas and Thanksgiving. In 1941, Zorn got the idea to sell turkeys throughout the year. Friends and family told him that he would lose his shirt. Zorn was determined and purchased two thousand poults, or baby turkeys, for the Bethpage farm. Unfortunately, he discovered that wholesale buyers offered less money for the birds than it cost to raise them, and so the retail establishment was born. Turkeys were plucked by hand, eviscerated and sold "oven ready" with no feet or head, versus the traditional manner, which was plucked with head and feet attached. In 1946, the family purchased a plucking machine and, in 1949, a rotisserie

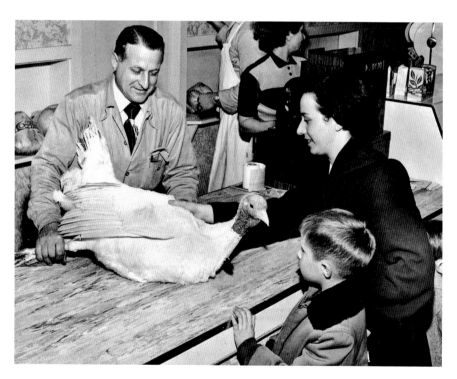

Peter Zorn began his retail poultry business more than seven decades ago. Undated. *Courtesy Zorn's of Bethpage.*

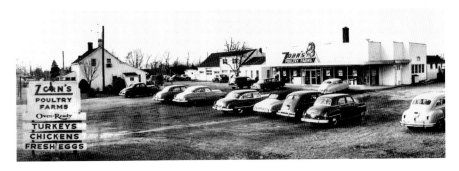

Zorn's has been located on Hempstead Turnpike in Bethpage since 1940. Undated. *Courtesy Zorn's of Bethpage.*

machine, and they offered a full home-style menu of fresh turkey and chicken, gravy, coleslaw, potato salad, macaroni salad and French fries.

In the late 1940s, the Grumman Aerospace Corporation (a large employer on Long Island and eventually famous as the company that designed the Apollo Lunar Module that landed on the moon) asked Peter Zorn to provide holiday turkeys for its employees. Zorn packaged the turkeys in decorated gift boxes. By the 1960s, in addition to his retail business, Zorn was selling twenty-five thousand turkeys just to corporations alone. The company provides holiday turkeys to Grumman—now known as Northrop Grumman Corporation—to this day. By the 1950s, Zorn's popular holiday catering menu was requested by customers throughout the year, and the Zorn family pioneered the concepts of full-service catering and convenient, complete takeout meals for busy suburban families.

Always an innovator, Peter Zorn continued to tinker with his recipe for success, working to breed the perfect turkey to meet the needs of his clientele. "He had a special white feather turkey and a Beltsville white and kept cross breeding them until he had a turkey with big breasts and a small cavity," said Merrill. "He bred it until he got to the turkey that he really wanted."

It was always, and is to this day, a family business. Merrill's father, Joseph, operated the Bethpage location for many years. Merrill now presides over the original retail store in Bethpage, and her brother, Peter, heads up a second retail store in Bellmore. The recipes for the extensive menu—first created by Peter and Gesine Zorn—are closely held. One might choose from a turkey feast, complete with stuffing, gravy and three large sides; a chicken and rib combo; a "bucket o' breasts"; or a comforting chicken potpie.

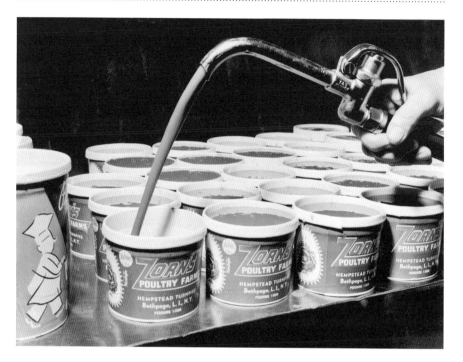

A staff member at Zorn's fills gravy cartons for sale. Undated. *Courtesy Zorn's of Bethpage.*

"All of our recipes are original," said Merrill. "Everything is made from scratch. We still hand-peel our potatoes, and there is nothing that comes processed. Every little thing that is put into every recipe is made from scratch as if you were cooking it at home." Mashed sweet potatoes, garlic mashed potatoes, creamed spinach and stuffing are enduring customer favorites.

A massive cobalt blue turkey still graces the façade of Zorn's. The original poultry farms have long since closed, and now all poultry is contract-grown to Zorn's specifications. Merrill continues to draw on family traditions as she shapes the business for the twenty-first century. Several years back, she resurrected a cartoon turkey that Peter Zorn used in his newspaper advertising, named him Earl and featured him in Zorn's social media efforts.

Peter Zorn's homemade approach requires a commitment that can be costly and time consuming. The Bethpage location employs a staff of sixty people who, among other tasks, peel potatoes by hand, roll dough for pie and mix spices daily. "We're still rolling out dough," laughed Merrill. "No one does what we do!"

She is constantly looking at how she must adapt her business model to meet the needs of customers and economic demands, but she believes that preserving what her grandfather began is worth the effort. "I hold true to our values and our traditions," said Merrill. "The customer is everything. I love feeding Long Island."

Zorn's of Bethpage
4321 Hempstead Turnpike
Bethpage, NY, 11714
516-731-5500
zornsonline.com

Chapter 9
Spirits, Brews and Beverages

D on't be misled by the proliferation of beer distributors, liquor marts and soda machines to be found on Long Island. While there is ample access to mass-produced beverages, Long Island is also home to a growing number of craft beverages—some wholly new and others firmly modeled on tradition.

For Long Island's early residents, quenching the thirst was a practical matter. Water was often contaminated, so colonists needed alternative beverages that stored well. These were typically made from items grown on the farm. Colonists drank distilled spirits and hard cider or imported fortified wines such as Madeira that required no refrigeration. When wine was produced, it was often a homemade affair using wild grapes. The wine was serviceable but did not match the quality of European varietals. Tea, coffee and chocolate were expensive, non-alcoholic options.

Today more than ever, "locally grown" is a standard ingredient in the tumbler, wine glass or growler, as adventurous Long Island artisans seek new inspiration for the libations we love. Craft beer is wildly popular, with more than fifteen microbreweries in Nassau and Suffolk Counties. At more than forty years old, the region known as Long Island Wine Country has come into its own, offering outstanding vintages of many varietals including Merlot and Cabernet Franc. A spirited distillery on Long Island's East End offers handcrafted vodka, gin, bourbon and rye that reflect Long Island's colorful past. There's always the autumnal option to quaff a glass of tart, fresh cider, pressed from Long Island apples. And for those who like to celebrate both special and everyday occasions, the presence of a winery on the East End devoted exclusively to sparkling wine is an effervescent delight.

JERICHO CIDER MILL

As fall leaves change to bronze and gold, cars queue up on Route 106 at the Jericho Cider Mill, with customers hoping to stock up on jugs of freshly pressed apple cider. As you walk to the storefront, try and resist the maze of rustic wooden crates overflowing with perfect green, red and gold New York State apples.

Tucked alongside a busy thoroughfare, the unassuming white clapboard building dates back to 1920. George Zulkofske's family purchased the cider mill in 1930. Zulkofske took over operation of the mill in 1970. For decades, Zulkofske was known as "Apple George." The mill is a relic of agricultural and estate life on Long Island. Cider mills were used to maximize the value and preserve an abundant apple crop. When the

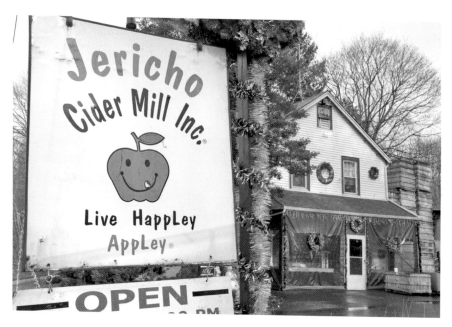

The Jericho Cider Mill has sold freshly pressed apple cider for more than seventy years. *Photo by John Barritt.*

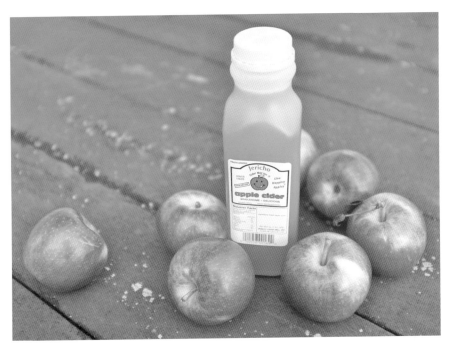

The apple cider at the Jericho Cider Mill draws crowds throughout autumn. *Photo by John Barritt.*

mill was first built, local farmers from Gold Coast estates in the area would trade apples for pressed cider. The Zulkofske family researched the location and found evidence of apple cider production at several spots on the site, dating back to the 1800s, including a mill that produced sparkling apple wine prior to Prohibition.

The family uses a German-built wine press to extract the fresh apple juice. Only fresh apples harvested in New York State and Long Island are used, and the cider contains no additional additives or preservatives. The cider tastes bright and clean, with a crisp apple aroma. The flavor and composition can change depending on the time of year and type of apples used. Cider extracted from the press is often more tart at the beginning of the apple harvest, but it might have a much higher sugar content when apples harvested near Thanksgiving are pressed.

The Jericho Cider Mill inspires fond smiles and memories from former and current residents of Long Island, and most everyone would endorse the mill's motto: "Live HappLey AppLey." In addition to fresh cider, customers can purchase homemade pies, breads and bags of fresh apples by the pound.

Jericho Cider Mill
213 Route 106
Jericho, NY, 11753
516-433-3360

LONG ISLAND WINE COUNTRY

The vineyards that thrive on the eastern end of Long Island infused new vitality into an agricultural region in transition. One can drive past mile after mile of neatly planted, plush vines that seem to roll on into eternity. Some are heavy with clusters of ebony grapes, while others shimmer with luminescent green orbs. To catch a few moments of sun-drenched solitude on a rustic deck overlooking the vineyards—with a glass of clean, crisp Long Island Chardonnay in hand—can provoke a sense of sublime pleasure.

When you witness the autumnal ritual of tourist-filled buses and limousines maneuvering on the narrow Main Road on Long Island's North Fork or the throngs of visitors from New York City clustered around sleek tasting bars housed in beautifully refurbished potato barns, it's easy to assume that the three thousand acres known as Long Island Wine Country sprang to life fully realized, the outcome of a brilliantly conceived and perfectly executed economic development plan. It all began with just one family farm and a husband and wife with a passion for hard work and the enchanting complexity of European-style wines.

Alex and Louisa Hargrave had no experience as farmers or vintners when they planted the first commercial *vinifera*—the European species of vine that yields classic wine grape varieties—on seventeen acres of a centuries-old potato farm in the town of Cutchogue in 1973. Now credited with pioneering an industry, the Hargraves were far from entrepreneurs. At the time, they were simply a young married couple pursuing their hopes and dreams and working to build a sustainable life for their family.

In her 2003 memoir, *The Vineyard*, Louisa Hargrave explained that the couple had only romantic notions about winemaking and a textbook on viticulture to guide them. Many thought that they were on a fool's errand. For centuries, farmers had tried and failed to cultivate *vinifera* on the East Coast, usually losing the battle with the cold winters. The Hargraves researched opportunities to establish vineyards on the West Coast and in the New York Finger Lakes region, but they were drawn to the North Fork in part because

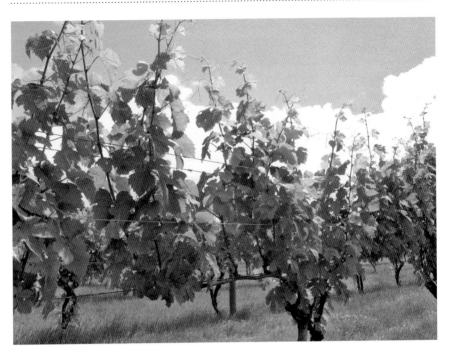

Macari Vineyards is one of sixty vineyards found on Long Island. *Photo by T.W. Barritt.*

of family connections and a belief that the climate would be favorable for growing grapes. The warmth from the ocean water that surrounds the North Fork creates a temperate climate and extends the summer growing season into autumn. The Hargraves believed that the fruit would have ample opportunity to ripen on the vine.

The first vines planted were Pinot Noir, Cabernet Sauvignon and Sauvignon Blanc. The Hargraves had to contend with mildew, contrary weather and fierce natural predators, but through constant tending of the vineyard, trial and error and a sheer sense of purpose, they prevailed. Hargrave Vineyards released its first commercial vintage in 1975. They had defied the odds and learned what was required to grow *vinifera* successfully. Wine enthusiasts and investors soon followed in their wake. As potato farmers were retiring, the land was purchased and converted into vineyards, and a new wine region emerged. By 1999, the Hargraves' marriage had dissolved, and they had sold the now eighty-four-acre vineyard to Marco and Ann Marie Borghese, who renamed the property Castello di Borghese Vineyard.

The original vines that the Hargraves planted by hand in 1973 are still tended today, and winemaking on Long Island has grown exponentially.

According to the Long Island Wine Council, there are more than sixty vineyards on Long Island, most on land once farmed by original settlers. The majority of vineyards are situated on the North Fork, with a handful on the South Fork and several in western Suffolk County. In 2015, the Long Island Wine Council reported annual production of 500,000 cases, which equals 1.2 million gallons. There are three appellations—or American Viticultural Areas (AVA), which are winegrowing regions defined by geography and climate. These include the North Fork, the Hamptons and the broader appellation of Long Island. According to United States guidelines, 85 percent of the grapes in a wine labeled with a specific AVA must come from that region. Long Island Wine Country has inspired a burgeoning tourism industry with farm stands, high-end restaurants and hotels benefiting from the influx of visitors in the past decade. Macari Vineyards, McCall Vineyards and Sparkling Pointe Winery regularly take top honors at the New York State Wine and Food Classic. In 2013, Long Island Wine Country was named one of the "Top Ten Wine Regions of the World" by *Wine Enthusiast* magazine.

Long Island Wine Council
5120 Sound Avenue
PO Box 600
Riverhead, NY, 11901
liwines.com

SPARKLING POINTE WINERY

Lovers of the bubbly have reason to celebrate. Long Island Wine Country has the distinction of being the home to Sparkling Pointe, the only winery in New York State dedicated to the exclusive production of Méthode Champenoise sparkling wine. Sparkling Pointe is a labor of love from husband and wife Thomas and Cynthia Rosicki, Long Island attorneys who love champagne and aspired to own a vineyard on the North Fork. When the opportunity to purchase a ten-acre parcel of land presented itself in 2004, the Rosickis decided to dedicate their future vineyard to their passion for sparkling wine.

The sleek, sophisticated tasting house—decorated in elegant pearl gray and white—suggests the pleasures that await visitors. The spacious tasting room is flanked by a long bar at one end and a fireplace at the other. Above the mantel, bottles of Sparkling Pointe's award-winning wines are displayed.

Beyond the fireplace is the smaller, more intimate "Bubble Room," available for private parties.

The Rosickis hired Gilles Martin, an award-winning wine expert born just outside the Champagne region in France, to guide their new venture. Educated in oenology at the prestigious University of Montpellier in France, Martin has traveled the world, working at wineries in Germany, Australia, California and the Rhone Valley. Eventually, in 1997, Martin came to Long Island, where he guided the development of the Macari, Martha Clara and Sherwood House Wineries.

Sparkling Pointe marketing and social media coordinator Kelsey Cheslock said that Martin believes the East End climate is ideal for growing the varietals used in sparkling wine. "He always thought that Long Island had a very similar climate to Champagne," said Cheslock. "It's a maritime climate

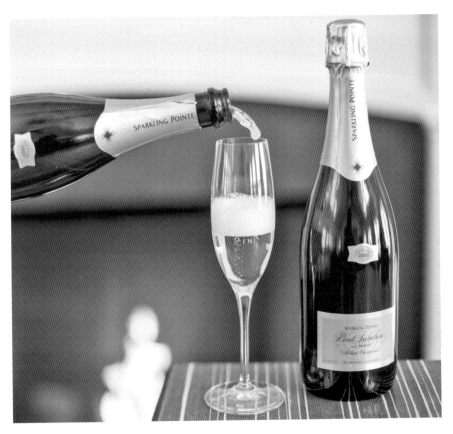

Sparkling Pointe is Long Island's only Méthode Champenoise–style winery. *Photo by Jacob Skoglund.*

with warm days and cool nights and that nice breeze that comes off from the bay side and the sound side."

The first vines were planted in 2004, and that same year, Sparkling Pointe released its first vintage, using fruit sourced from other North Fork vineyards. The first harvest and vintage from estate-grown fruit was released in 2007. Cheslock noted that today, thirty-four acres are planted with the traditional champagne varietal grapes that include Chardonnay, Pinot Noir and Pinot Meunier. The winery houses sixteen stainless steel tanks and produces approximately 4,500 cases of sparkling wine annually. Only the region of Champagne can use that name for sparkling wines. Wines produced outside Champagne, France, must be referred to as sparkling wines. Sparkling Pointe is the only winery in New York State that uses the double-fermentation process, or the "Méthode Champenoise," used in France.

The accolades continue to mount. Sparkling Pointe 2005 Brut Seduction—a 57 percent Pinot Noir, 43 percent Chardonnay blend—was awarded Best Sparkling Wine in New York State, Double Gold at the 2014 New York Wine and Food Classic. The 2011 Topaz Imperial—a light pink blend of 50 percent Chardonnay, 40 percent Pinot Noir and 10 percent Pinot Meunier—was awarded a ninety-point score by *Wine Enthusiast*.

Cheslock said that the Rosickis are thrilled with the public and profession's response to the winery. "This is their pride and joy," she said. "They love telling the story of Sparkling Pointe and love spreading the message."

Sparkling Pointe hosts imaginative pairing events designed to match its sparkling wines with products such as New York artisanal confections, French-style macarons, cupcakes and international cheeses. "We're really focused on the education," said Cheslock. "We want people to leave here knowing what Méthode Champenoise means and knowing how you make sparkling wine."

Sparkling Pointe Winery
39750 Country Road 48
Southold, NY, 11971
631-765-0200
sparklingpointe.com

Long Island Spirits

Long Island Spirits in Baiting Hollow is billed as Long Island's first craft distillery and is often referred to as the first distillery in the region since the 1800s. To hear founder Rich Stabile tell it, stills were at one time standard equipment on most farms. "Everyone had a still before Prohibition and maybe even some during," he noted. "It was kind of a common thing, and that's what you did with your excess crops. There were a lot of personal distilling projects as an adjunct to farming activities."

The establishment of Long Island Spirits in 2007 as the first professional distillery on the East End was a game changer in what was already an established region for wine. The distillery and tasting room for Long Island Spirits is housed in a rustic barn constructed by a Polish immigrant family in the early 1900s. They grew potatoes on the land until 1943. The building is surrounded by some five thousand acres of potato farms.

Perhaps it's no surprise that when Stabile opened for business, his flagship product was LiV Vodka, distilled from 100 percent Long Island potatoes. The cool blue bottle evokes a sense of the Long Island seashore. The award-winning vodka is distilled in small batches from locally farmed Marcy Russet potatoes. Stabile said that the Long Island potato has a perfect starch

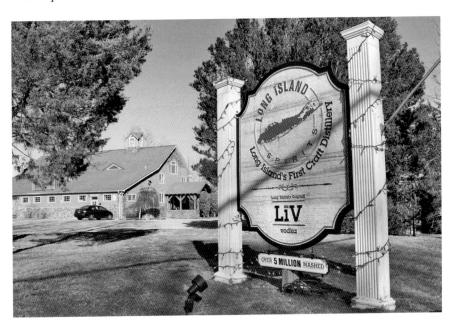

Long Island Spirits is Long Island's first craft distillery since the 1800s. *Photo by Jacob Skoglund.*

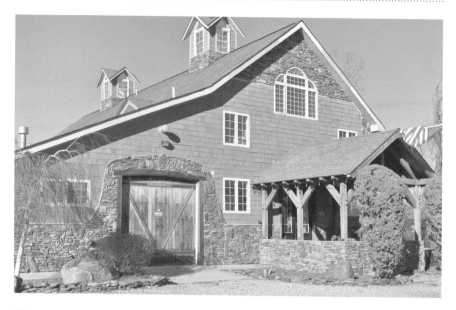

The Long Island Spirits tasting room was once a barn that stored potatoes. *Photo by Jacob Skoglund.*

content for producing vodka, which results in distinctive tasting notes of vanilla, citrus, anise and a creamy mouth feel not found in the typical vodka distilled from grain.

Stabile's first product extension was his line of Sorbetta liqueurs. Sorbetta uses LiV Vodka as a base and adds hand-peeled and macerated fresh fruits for a vibrant and flavorful liqueur. Sorbetta is available in lemon, lime, orange, raspberry and strawberry.

A walk through the stylish tasting room above the distillery—which is open seven days a week—is like exploring a scrapbook of Long Island times gone by. Stabile continues to expand his product line, exploring new spirits and styles and using Long Island heroes, geology and imagery as inspiration. He hopes the various brands evoke a strong sense of place. "I've got long, strong ties with Long Island. I've got a lot of hometown pride and wanted to pick different names for different brands that would conjure up an emotional impulse."

Pine Barrens Single Malt Whisky is named for the Suffolk County Central Pine Barrens region, an area of more than 100,000 acres of protected pine forests and wetlands. It was the first American single-malt whiskey to be distilled on Long Island and uses a barley wine English-style ale beer as its base.

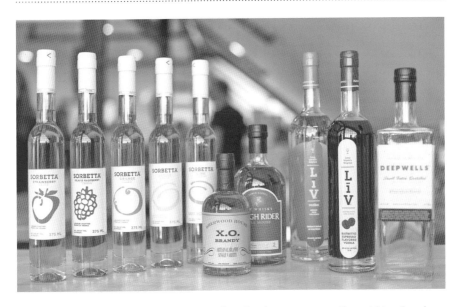

Long Island Spirits offers craft vodka made from local potatoes, as well as whiskey, bourbon, rye and specialty liquors. *Photo by Jacob Skoglund.*

Rough Rider Straight Bourbon Whisky and Rough Rider Bull Moose Three Barrel Rye Whisky honor Oyster Bay resident Teddy Roosevelt and the Rough Riders, the volunteer cavalry fighting unit that gained fame at the Battle of San Juan Hill. Roosevelt and the Rough Riders quarantined and later disbanded at Camp Wikoff at Montauk Point in 1898 following their return from the Spanish-American War. "Roosevelt was one of my favorite presidents, and I love his pioneering spirit," said Stabile. "He was a Renaissance man, which I thought was very appropriate for whiskey."

Rough Rider Straight Bourbon Whisky is an aged bourbon mash of 60 percent corn, 35 percent rye and 5 percent barley aged in new charred American oak barrels. Rough Rider Bull Moose Rye uses a three-barrel aging method.

LiV Vodka is the base for Long Island Spirits' first foray into gin. Deepwells Botanical Gin is distilled in small batches, infusing the base spirit of potato vodka with twenty-eight local and exotic botanicals. It promises notes of citrus, florals and juniper. The water source for the gin comes from the glacial aquifer found in the Central Pine Barrens region, which geologists referred to as "deepwells," according to Stabile.

Long Island Spirits mixologists design a variety of craft cocktail recipes that make the most of Rich Stabile's signature spirits. The Long Island

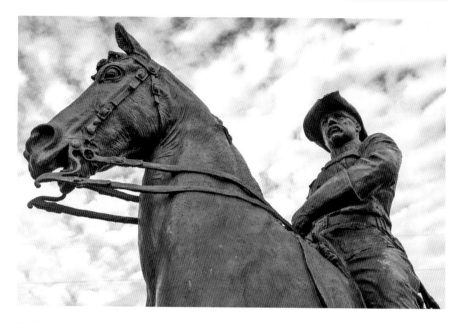

Teddy Roosevelt is the inspiration for bourbon and rye crafted by Long Island Spirits in Baiting Hollow. *Photo by John Barritt.*

Sound cocktail evokes a summer day on the North Shore of Long Island, and Teddy's Revenge inspires the "take no prisoners" attitude of the twenty-sixth president of the United States.

Long Island Sound

1½ ounces LiV Vodka

2 ounces coconut water

⅓ ounce Sorbetta Lime

¼ ounce simple syrup

1 teaspoon lime zest

Shake all ingredients, strain over ice and pour into a double rocks glass. Garnish with a lime wheel.

Teddy's Revenge

4 fresh mint sprigs
1 teaspoon powdered sugar
2 teaspoons water
2½ parts Rough Rider Straight Bourbon Whisky

Muddle mint leaves, powdered sugar and water in a Collins glass. Fill the glass with crushed ice and add bourbon. Top with more ice and garnish with a mint sprig.

Long Island Spirits
2182 Sound Avenue
Baiting Hollow, NY, 11933
631-630-9322
lispirits.com

OYSTER BAY BREWING COMPANY

Gabe Haim and Ryan Schlotter—owners of the Oyster Bay Brewing Company—enjoy talking about local icons. It is not long before Teddy Roosevelt, a renowned resident of Oyster Bay, enters the conversation. "Just down the road is Snouders Drug Store," said Haim, referring to an old-time soda fountain in town. "You'd go in and fill up on soda. Teddy Roosevelt used to take phone calls there. He would summer here in Oyster Bay, and they called Sagamore Hill the Summer White House."

Haim and Schlotter are creating their own icon: the first craft brewery on Long Island's Gold Coast, located in one of Long Island's most historic towns. They point out that they use Oyster Bay water to brew their beer, and the site of the original town spring where residents would fill their jugs is just steps away from their location. "You can come here and fill a growler with beer, just like in the past you could come here and get a refill at the soda fountain," said Haim. "So it's a nice tie to history."

The two Long Island natives are in their early thirties. They started brewing as a hobby but now find themselves at the center of a rapidly growing craft beer movement on Long Island. "We have a great local following," said

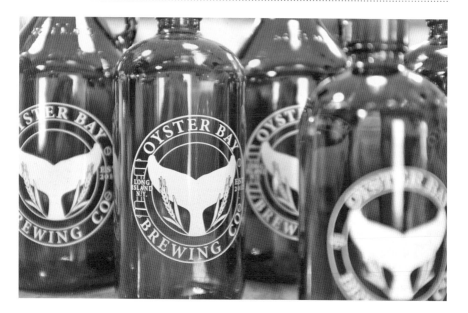

Growlers to be filled at the Oyster Bay Brewing Company. *Photo by John Barritt.*

Haim. "The cool thing with craft beer is that it's so hot right now. A regular thing to do on a weekend is to go to a brewery and do a tasting."

Between the mid-nineteenth and early twentieth centuries, there was a plethora of breweries operating in Brooklyn, but it wasn't until the Blue Point Brewing Company was established in Patchogue in 1997 that central Long Island would become a hub for craft brewing. Today, there are nearly thirty craft microbreweries and brewpubs on Long Island. Haim and Schlotter seem to relish the fact that they are engaged in an age-old tradition. "Making beer has been around for thousands of years," said Haim. "It's a very old process that hasn't changed. Beer is made with four ingredients—barley, hops, water and yeast—so you're true to that process. What we're making is a very old, ancient product, and what we do is historical."

The operation includes a small brewery and tasting room. Customers can see the steel brewing tanks, sample beer on tap and fill reusable amber-colored glass bottles called "growlers" to take beer home. The small operation brews two to three times a week and produced about four hundred barrels of beer and lager in 2014.

The simple stucco building where Haim and Schlotter opened for business in June 2013 had its own enticing history. While more recently a garishly painted Mexican restaurant, it was once connected with local law enforcement. "This building used to be an old jail," explained Haim, "back

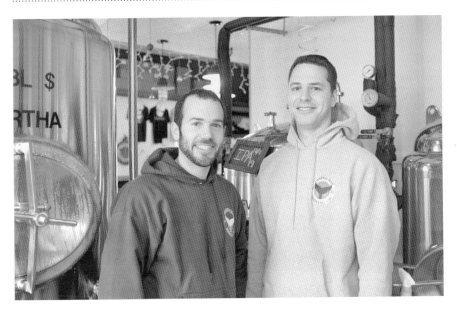

Gabe Haim and Ryan Schlotter founded the Oyster Bay Brewing Company. *Photo by John Barritt.*

in the early 1900s, and they used to put prisoners on the train from Oyster Bay to the Mineola jail." Downstairs in the basement, there is a room with two windows and metal bars that used to contain two holding cells.

"We use it as the drunk tank for nasty customers and bad tippers," joked Schlotter.

A home brewing kit was the catalyst for their business venture. "We just started messing around," said Haim. "I made a batch at home, and he made a batch at home and then we started making it together."

As you listen to the quick-witted rapport between Haim and Schlotter, it is easy to imagine the two affable guys as the stars of a buddy movie on craft brewing. In fact, once the duo had decided on their future business partnership, they actually took a road trip together to learn the art of craft brewing. "You find out a lot about each other on the road," deadpanned Schlotter.

They are constantly experimenting with their selection of craft beers, brewing customer favorites and limited editions. "Our goal from the beginning has been to stay true to the craft beer world but, at the same time, make all of our beers very drinkable for the average beer drinker and the flavors very noticeable for the craft beer drinker," said Schlotter.

"There are so many different variables that you can work with and change when you're making beer," added Schlotter. "I think we learn something different every day. You're tailoring everything, and in that process a lot of creation happens."

Their menu has included imperial IPA, honey ale, amber ale, wheat ale, pale ale, stout and, during winter months, a Spiced Holiday Surprise. "We did a limited-release Oyster Stout when we did a partnership fundraiser with the Baymen's association," said Schlotter. "They donated the oysters and shucked them, and we made a stout that we sunk some oysters into and it was very popular."

"It was a very local beer, and all the oysters came from Oyster Bay," said Haim. "It gave it a briny saltiness that people were looking for. It was pretty cool."

They even launched a special craft brew called Barn Rocker in honor of the New York Islanders, which was available on tap at the Nassau Coliseum during the 2015 season.

The team keeps finding ways to make the business more sustainable. They've launched a very popular brand of homemade doggie treats made from the used hops. They also have a barter arrangement with local farms that use spent grain for chicken feed and compost.

Haim and Schlotter bonded over their love of beer and burgeoning business, but they've also become local ambassadors making a bit of beverage history in one of Long Island's most notable towns. "It's nice to have a new business in a very hot industry that brings a lot of people to the town," said Haim.

Despite the potential burden of the responsibility, they're not taking themselves too seriously. "We have too much fun," said Haim. "It's not fair."

In the spring of 2015, Oyster Bay Brewing Company announced an expansion and move to a larger location close to its original tasting room.

Oyster Bay Brewing Company
36 Audrey Avenue
Oyster Bay, NY, 11771
516-802-5546
oysterbaybrewing.com

WOODSIDE HARD CIDER

It is a clear and bracingly crisp winter Saturday afternoon on the North Fork of Long Island. Layers of snow and ice surround a brilliant, apple-red barn that sits on the Main Road in Aquebogue. It is the home of Woodside Orchards. The interior of the barn is raw wood beams and paneling. There is a palpable chill in the air, but it is kept at bay by a sense of warm conviviality. People are crowded together in the tasting room, wearing their winter coats, laughing and quaffing hard cider poured from the tap. The craft cidery has caught on so quickly with the community that there hasn't been much time to insulate the structure that was originally designed as a seasonal farm stand for the autumn apple harvest.

An increasingly popular drink in the United States and Canada, hard cider is a relatively new venture for Long Island, but it is rooted in the farming practices of the region. Apples are found in abundance on Long Island, and New York State is the nation's second-largest producer of apples. Historically, most working farms would have had an apple tree on site if not a full orchard. Long Island even claims the birthright of a venerable heritage apple variety. The Green Newtown Pippin apple was a bit of a happy accident that first sprouted from a random apple seed and was harvested in 1730 in Newtown, Queens County (today known as Elmhurst). The Newtown Pippin was believed to be the preferred apple of George Washington and Thomas Jefferson, who cultivated the variety at his Monticello estate. The variety was more broadly commercialized in the nineteenth century.

Today, Long Island is home to scores of pick-your-own apple orchards that attract thousands of visitors each autumn. Wickham's Fruit Farm in Cutchogue dates to 1661 and includes some of the oldest continually cultivated farmland in the United States. It offers summer and autumn apples for picking.

Hard cider—a practical, utilitarian drink—has been produced for centuries. Yeast occurs naturally on apples and can ferment apple juice that sits at room temperature. The English brought hard cider to America. It was a popular drink in the northeastern colonies, where apples thrived, and it stored well for long periods. Hard cider production would have been common among local farmers looking for ways to utilize and preserve the apple harvest. For the owners of Woodside Orchards, their foray into hard cider has helped fuel a year-round business.

"We were making a good living for quite a few years just with the u-pick model, and it went very well, but it's a seasonal business," said co-owner Bob Gammon. "You pad your checkbook, and then come December you hemorrhage money all winter long. We were looking for something apple-based that would extend the season."

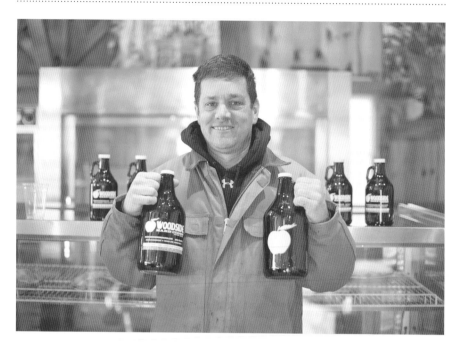

Bob Gammon of Woodside Orchards uses winemaking techniques to produce hard cider. *Photo by Jacob Skoglund.*

Woodside Orchards began as a family-owned, pick-your-own apple orchard in the early 1980s. It offers twenty-eight different varieties of apples, available to be picked throughout the autumn season, including historic favorites such as the Baldwin and Golden Russet and the Jonathan, a two-hundred-year-old variety from New York State. Visitors can also choose from a selection of pies and baked goods prepared on site, as well as honey and an acclaimed fresh cider sold each autumn. Several Long Island wineries have dabbled in hard cider in recent years, and there are several fresh cider mills, but Woodside Orchards is the only craft hard cidery on Long Island using apples harvested on site. The sharp, white logo that marks the Woodside Hard Cider growlers makes the claim of ownership—an apple with a stem and a leaf that graphically depicts the landmass of Long Island.

"A hard cider is very similar to a wine," said Gammon. "Essentially, you're taking fruit and adding yeast and fermenting it. The yeast consumes the sugar in the fruit and turns it to alcohol."

The family worked closely with a local winemaking expert to develop their product. A farm winery license allows the family to produce the hard cider as long as they grow the apples on site. Six to eight apple varieties are used to achieve the desired sugar content in the juice. The choice of yeast is critical to the final product. Some yeast consumes more sugar, resulting in dry cider. Others consume less sugar, producing a sweeter cider. The hard cider is fermented in tanks over six to eight weeks. The product is force-carbonated prior to serving. Woodside Orchards' first limited release was announced in November 2012.

On this winter day, there are four styles of Woodside Hard Cider listed in chalk on the blackboard above the bar and available on tap. Traditional Cider is dry, bright and brisk. Traditional Sweet Cider has just a touch more sugar. Raspberry Cider is pleasantly pink and refreshing. Cinnamon Cider is laced with warm, autumnal spices. Woodside Orchards also offers limited seasonal releases, such as apple pumpkin cider and apple ginger cider. Refillable glass growlers are available in various sizes. The reception from the community has exceeded the owners' expectations.

"You never know where life's going to take you," said Gammon. "I went to school for criminology and sociology, and now I'm an apple-peddling bartender, so go figure."

Woodside Orchards
729 Main Road, Route 25
Aquebogue, NY, 11931
631-722-5770
woodsideorchards.com

Woodside Orchards (seasonal location)
116 Manor Lane
Jamesport, NY, 11947

Chapter 10
Classic Roadside Joints

Ever since the controversial master builder Robert Moses completed his first highway, Long Island has been a car culture. An automobile is standard issue for the far-flung suburban lifestyle. Nineteen major highways connect Long Island, and by some shocking estimates, we own an average of 3.4 cars per household. That's bad news for the carbon footprint and certainly makes getting from point A to point B a daily traffic nightmare.

The Long Island Expressway—officially known as Interstate 495—is the main highway that stretches from west to east for nearly seventy miles linking New York City with Riverhead in Suffolk County. For better or worse, the highway system was a necessity as Long Island was developed, but it killed a certain inherent small-town quality now only evident when one travels to the North Fork.

We Long Islanders keep a tight schedule, and we love to jump in the car and go! Food has to be convenient to those for whom their automobile is a second home, and plenty of fast-food chains and pizzerias are ready to serve up sustenance. In between the highways and endless traffic lights, though, you can also discover the existence of authentic roadside joints with colorful backstories, complete with gravel parking lots, picnic tables and just enough noise pollution to make things interesting. Some operate seasonally and cater to the summer traveler, and some have established year-round operations, but the menu is always stick-to-your-ribs good. So, when you've had your fill of kale and kohlrabi, take a ride in the car across Long Island. There's still a roadside joint or drive-in for every taste.

ALL AMERICAN HAMBURGER DRIVE-IN

A cavalcade of cars, carbohydrates and crowds is the best way to describe the daily action at the All American Hamburger Drive-In in Massapequa. Established in 1963 by Philip Vultaggio, the gleaming, space-aged drive-in with the patriotic red, white and blue logo has shown amazing staying power for more than half a century.

Fans begin lining up to place orders just after breakfast, and the pace doesn't quiet down until late evening. It can be a challenge to maneuver the vestibule and place an order. It's a bit like navigating the New York City subway system on a busy morning, but those who figure it out are rewarded quickly with steaming sacks of freshly prepared hamburgers, fries and thick, creamy shakes. Now operated by Vultaggio's sons, William and Philip, All American seems to employ a battalion of young kitchen staffers in white uniforms who turn around an order and satisfy a craving lickety-split. There is limited outdoor seating on the patio, and none in the restaurant, but it doesn't seem to matter. This is not about ambiance. Patrons are perfectly happy to grab their burgers and get on their way or chow down right in the car.

The menu is classic burger joint fare. Is it better than the average national chain hamburger? The diehard fans seem to think so, and the price is right. In 2015, All American was selling hamburgers for $1.30, cheeseburgers for

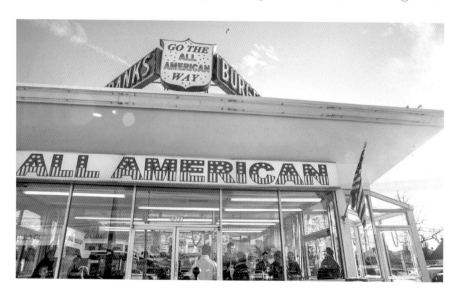

Massapequa's All American Hamburger Drive-In draws crowds daily. *Photo by Jacob Skoglund.*

$1.50 and double cheeseburgers for $2.85, with recipes that haven't changed for fifty years.

Perhaps the greatest reason folks keep coming back to All American is that everyone loves a hometown success story.

All American Hamburger Drive-In
4286 Merrick Road
Massapequa, NY, 11758
allamericanhamburgerli.com

FLO'S FAMOUS LUNCHEONETTE

Summer is officially underway when Flo's Famous Luncheonette opens for business in Blue Point around Memorial Day weekend. Serving burgers, wraps, salads and seafood daily, only through Labor Day, the joys of Flo's are as fleeting as a summer ice cream cone but well worth the experience. Florence Kimball opened her luncheonette in 1926, serving "toasted sandwiches" to local patrons. The roadside eatery had hatch windows, a

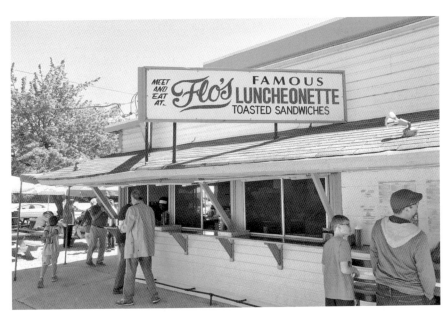

Flo's Famous Luncheonette in Blue Point opened for business in 1926. *Photo by T.W. Barritt.*

lunch counter and a large, welcoming sign that invited the community to "Meet and Eat at Flo's." Mrs. Kimball passed away in 1950, and subsequent owners have kept her spirit of hospitality alive with classic menu items like the Flo Burger, the Flo Dog and Flo's Special—Canadian bacon, lettuce and tomato on toast.

There's no denying the satisfying goodness of a towering grilled sandwich, topped with bread that literally glows with a golden, toasted patina. Burgers are thick and juicy; bacon and cheese are compulsory toppings. The French fries are so crisp they crackle.

Flo's owners have created a dockside at roadside. Just a short walk to the ocean, the sparkling-white siding and smart nautical-blue trim evoke a relaxing day at the beach. Two model lighthouses flank the counter window. If you're in a hurry, chill out—it's the beach. The service is leisurely, and the clean-cut staff is friendly and attentive.

At nearly ninety years old, Flo's still manages to keep up with the times, launching a roving food truck in 2013 and a year-round restaurant in Patchogue in 2014 and maintaining a social media presence.

Flo's Famous Luncheonette
302 Middle Road
Blue Point, NY, 11715
888-FLOS-TOGO
flosfamous.com

BIGELOW'S

Two steely matrons walk into a venerable Rockville Centre seafood diner on a glorious spring day. They are clearly regulars, but it's their first visit since the spring thaw, and it has been a long, cold winter. One of them asks the counter guy, "What's new on the menu?"

He shrugs. "Things don't change here," he replies with a smile.

In the case of Bigelow's, that kind of dependability is what has kept customers returning for more than seventy-five years. Russ Bigelow opened his self-named seafood restaurant on a quiet corner in Rockville Centre in 1939. The takeout menu points out that it was also the year the movie *Gone with the Wind* premiered. Bigelow had worked in hotels in New England and knew a thing or two about frying seafood. His signature dish was fried

Ipswich clams. When drenched in batter and submerged in a fryer, the soft-shell, whole belly clams become searing mouthfuls of crisp, buttery bliss.

Pass through the door of the tidy blue and white cottage, and you'll feel as if you've been transported to an old-time clam shack by the shore. Oddly enough, the restaurant is nowhere near salt water and sits on one of the busiest thoroughfares in Nassau County, surrounded by a train station, an optical franchise and assorted car dealerships. A wraparound green Formica counter seats about thirty people and affords a good view of the kitchen activity. Hearing those battered clams sizzle in hot oil adds a touch of ecstasy to the dining experience. Bigelow's has used the same recipe since 1939 and changes the fry oil daily, which clearly contributes to the fresh taste.

When Russ Bigelow first welcomed guests, the restaurant was only opened for the summer season. You can see evidence of where the original open takeout window ran parallel to the dining counter, but the entire area has since been enclosed.

The décor is shabby maritime chic, including ancient postcards and photos, conch shells and starfish, nautical memorabilia and even a classic Zenith portable TV. Don't miss the plaque with the motto, "Fresh Oysters, Beer on Ice, That's Paradise."

Bigelow's menu items are served direct from the fryer or the grill, piled high on deliciously no-frill paper plates. In addition to Russ Bigelow's famous Ipswich clams, one can choose from shrimp, bay scallops, New England clam chowder, seafood bisque, crab cakes, calamari, seafood platters and marinated fish prepared on the grill. And in a charming protest against modern electronic payments, Bigelow's only accepts cash, but it does have an ATM conveniently located on site just in case you find you are short a few bucks.

Bigelow's
79 North Long Beach Road
Rockville Centre, NY, 11570
516-678-3878
bigelows-rvc.com

The Shack

If you like your roadside joint with a healthy serving of street smarts, they've been serving up "clams and chaos" at the Shack in Centerport since 1980.

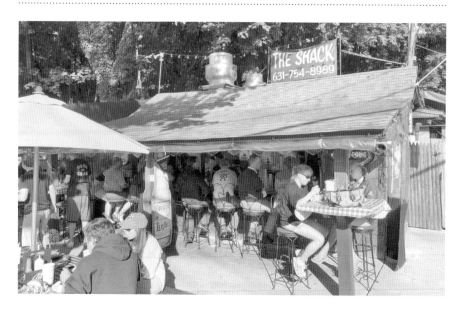

The Shack in Centerport is a classic Long Island summer road joint. *Photo by T.W. Barritt.*

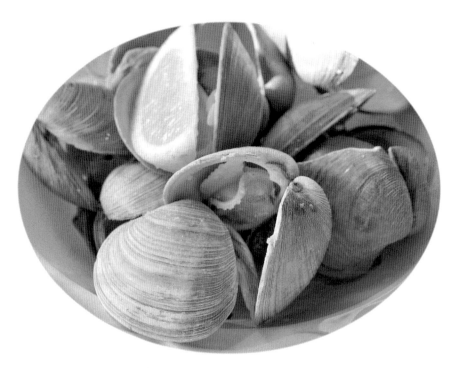

Steamed clams served at the Shack in Centerport. *Photo by T.W. Barritt.*

The weather-beaten, clapboard structure, built in 1927, is opened seasonally from May to October and is a mainstay of the summer al fresco season on the North Shore. Parking is tight, but the Shack is a haven for everyone from seniors to bikers and business tycoons, as the selection of Harley-Davidson motorcycles, Corvettes and BMWs attests. You can't beat the convenience to Route 25A. The Shack is about as "roadside" as you can get without dining in the intersection.

The owners have dubbed the Shack "the Tavern on the Gravel," but don't look for calculated elegance. Red-and-white checkered cloths adorn the picnic tables and a man-made waterfall adds a fleeting moment of serenity, but it's all about the chaotic vibe on which the kitchen team thrives. Orders move at a fast pace, and trays are piled high with steamed clams, burgers, fries and chubby lobster rolls. There's also a diverse selection of beers. It's a bit of a rush to sit on the gravel in the summer sun—with a plate of golden fried clams and a beer in hand—listening to the cacophony of orders being called and the traffic zipping by. The Shack is enduring proof that one man's ambiance is another man's adrenaline.

The Shack
1 Stony Hollow Road—25A
Centerport, NY, 11721
631-754-8989
theshack25a.com

Chapter 11
Fine Dining

From Historic to Haute Cuisine

The very concept of a restaurant is a relatively modern phenomenon on Long Island, yet the need for hospitality has existed for centuries. Entrepreneurs—who owned buildings located on established routes—knew that travelers needed a convenient place to rest and find food and drink. Some responded by opening their homes, while others founded more formal business enterprises.

One can still find remnants of Long Island's nascent hospitality industry today. At Old Bethpage Village Restoration, the Noon Inn appears much as it did in the 1850s. Built between 1831 and 1845 and operated by John Noon from 1848 to 1859, it is a good example of a Spartan structure that addressed an economic need. Originally located at the intersection of Prospect Avenue and East Meadow Avenue, it served as a respite for weary travelers.

Many historic venues have evolved over centuries yet retain a legacy of hospitality to this day. The upscale Jedediah Hawkins Inn in Jamesport, built in 1863, is the former home of a sea captain and partners closely with North Fork wineries. In Stony Brook, the colonial building that houses the restaurant Mirabelle at Three Village Inn was built in 1751 by Richard Hallock and called the Old Homestead. At times during its history, it was used as a summer residence before Mrs. Frank Melville purchased it in 1929 as a meeting place for women. She served tea, sandwiches and refreshments to her guests, and over time, the operation expanded to serve meals and provide overnight accommodations. Today, the four-star Restaurant Mirabelle at Three Village Inn serves local cuisine with French flair.

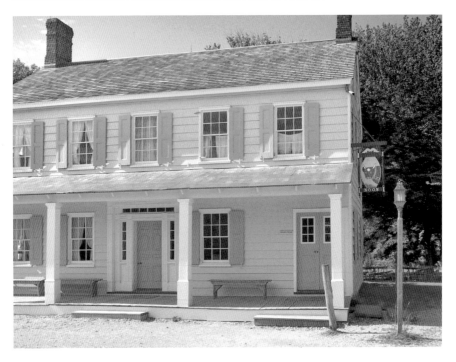

The Noon Inn, an original Long Island tavern. *Photo by T.W. Barritt.*

The Long Island restaurant of the twenty-first century has moved from practicality to pleasure. "Farm to table," once a way of life, has become a selling point. Celebrated chefs like Tom Schaudel of Jewel, Guy Reuge of Restaurant Mirabelle and Claudia Fleming of North Fork Table and Inn have forsaken the big city to establish enduring homes on Long Island and menus that feature the bounty of the region. Through their efforts and those of others, Long Island has become a culinary destination versus a brief stopover on a journey elsewhere.

Yet much like the taverns of old that connected travel routes, fine dining on Long Island is connecting guests to the significant agricultural resources found in the region, and it is even helping define how those resources will be grown in the future.

THE MILLERIDGE INN

Wedding showers, anniversary celebrations, baptisms, bar mitzvahs and elaborate Sunday brunches. That's the classic association one has with the sprawling, shingled colonial inn that sits atop a bluff at the crossroads of Jericho Turnpike and Route 106 in Jericho. For decades, many a family milestone has been marked at the venerable Milleridge Inn. While the food and dining ambiance might resemble banquet-style, country club fare, the history of the place is undeniable. The constant procession of relatives and friends bearing gifts belies the fact that the inn is the cradle of Long Island hospitality.

The history of the Milleridge Inn begins nearly a century before the American Revolutionary War. The year is 1672, and Mary Willet, a widow and Quaker minister, builds a small two-room house with a central fireplace near the spring pond in the region known as Jericho. She holds Quaker worship meetings in her home and welcomes travelers with meals and lodging. In later years, it is believed that the home is used to quarter British and Hessian troops during the Revolutionary War and as a stop on the Underground Railroad for slaves in pursuit of freedom. Mary Willet's two rooms and fireplace are the heart of the modern-day Milleridge Inn and can still be viewed inside the main entrance of the restaurant, although the size and footprint of the structure have changed dramatically.

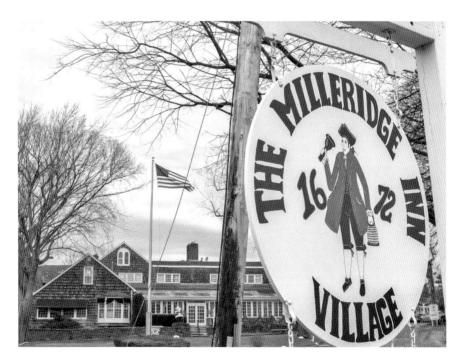

The Milleridge Inn first welcomed visitors in 1672. *Photo by John Barritt.*

Mary Willet's descendants continued her spirit of hospitality. In 1770, Quaker Elias Hicks married Jemima Seaman, the great-granddaughter of Mary Willet. At the conclusion of the Revolutionary War, the Hicks family opened their home in Jericho to travelers journeying along the busy thoroughfare at Jericho Road. The Hickses served stew, fish, meat and fresh-baked bread to their visitors. Travelers were invited to sleep by the hearth overnight, and the Hickses asked for no payment for services.

Mary Willet's original home continued to evolve over the centuries. A second story and additional rooms were added. By the start of the twentieth century, the location was well known as a dining establishment. Between 1930 and 1950, it was called the Maine Maid Inn before being renamed the Mille Ridge Restaurant. In 1963, the Murphy family purchased the restaurant and the surrounding ten acres and renamed the restaurant the Milleridge Inn. Today, the inn offers eleven dining rooms and a selection of period-style shops. The menu is classic American fare, featuring such stalwarts as Waldorf salad, Yankee pot roast, sauerbraten and baked stuffed shrimp.

The Milleridge Inn
585 North Broadway
Jericho, NY, 11753
516-931-2201
milleridge.com

RELISH

The giant overstuffed omelettes that headline the breakfast menu (served each day from 8:00 a.m. until 4:00 p.m.) at Relish in Kings Park are about as fresh and local as you can get. Most patrons might not realize that the eggs are sourced just five minutes down the road or that the busy intersection where Relish sits was once expansive farmland known locally as Indian Head.

Relish has upended the idea of the classic neighborhood diner and given it new meaning, featuring comfort food prepared with locally sourced ingredients. The restaurant is a sleek, high-end diner with swivel stools at the counter and olive-colored booths. Menu items are served in portion sizes that are reminiscent of an old-school diner, but the twist is that fruits, vegetables and eggs are sourced locally.

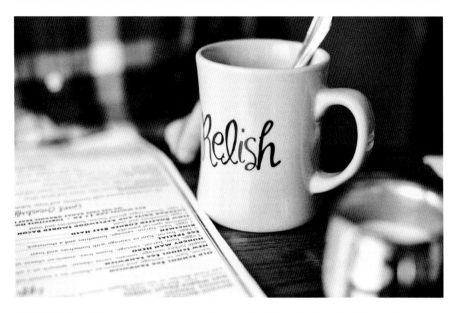

Relish in Kings Park uses eggs sourced from nearby Raleigh's Poultry Farm. *Photo by Jacob Skoglund.*

The idea of family seems a key ingredient in the success of Relish. The cordial waitstaff wear slate-gray T-shirts emblazoned with the slogan "Food, Family & Life." On weekends, families pour into the restaurant for enormous cups of coffee and hearty breakfast dishes made in a genuine farm-to-table arrangement with free-range organic eggs from the Raleigh's Poultry Farm and Country Store in Kings Park. Relish chef and co-owner Stephen Cardello cooks up an enticing menu of satisfying options, such as the Old School Egg Sandwich with ham and American cheese on a toasted roll; a Mexicali Omelette with homemade chorizo, onions, green chile and Jack cheese; or a Brooklyn Omelette with sweet fennel sausage, fire-roasted peppers, onions and provolone cheese.

For those interested in checking out the origin of their food, Raleigh's Poultry Farm and Country Store is tucked away at the top of the hill within a nearby suburban neighborhood. Sisters Cathy and Maura are the Raleigh daughters who were born and raised on the twenty-acre farm and are the caretakers of the enterprise that has operated for nearly sixty years. In addition to organic eggs, Raleigh's offers organic poultry, beef and pork, as well as organic dairy products and a selection of baked goods.

Relish
2 Pulaski Road
Kings Park, NY, 11754
631-292-2740
relishkingspark.com

Raleigh's Poultry Farm and Country Store
335 Old Indian Head Road
Kings Park, NY, 11754
631-269-4428

Market Bistro

Farm-to-table dining comes to the strip mall at Market Bistro in Jericho. Just a few steps away from the historic Milleridge Inn, Market Bistro is tucked into the quintessential twenty-first-century Long Island terrain. Surrounded by asphalt, a corporate office building, a discount clothing store, a nail salon and one of the only Whole Foods found in Nassau County, Market Bistro is a bit of a non sequitur. It's the kind of environment where you might expect to find Buffalo chicken wings and six-packs in abundant supply, yet Market Bistro advocates a strong alternative philosophy. Proprietors Bill Holden and Bob Caras are dedicated to creating a gateway for seasonal, locally sourced food in Nassau County.

The idea of "farm to table" in the heart of Jericho is not so far-fetched. Welshman Robert Williams purchased the land now known as Jericho in 1648 from the chief of the Matinecock Indian tribe. At the time, the area was known as Lusum, which many believe is an Indian word that meant "the farms." By 1692, the area had grown into a community of Quaker farmers. Families established homes around a local freshwater spring, and Williams called the area Jericho, as it was a Quaker tradition to name locations after places mentioned in the Bible. A nearby Indian trail that once ran all the way to Manhattan is now the modern-day, highly trafficked Jericho Turnpike.

Market Bistro is an intriguing hybrid of local community culture and Long Island's aspiring food scene. On a given night, one can observe families celebrating birthdays, a girls' night out and brawny guys hugging the bar and watching hockey on two large, flat-screen televisions. In fact, it is evident that the owners are assimilating a farm-to-table ethos into everyday meet-ups and celebrations.

Visitors to Market Bistro enter a soaring great room decorated with reclaimed wood, white tile and a rugged brick wall. A stack of wooden barrels divides the dining room and the kitchen. An expansive chalkboard has specials and local suppliers noted in big block letters.

Market Bistro lists Satur Farms in Cutchogue as a primary source of ingredients. One can find lush greens, heirloom tomatoes and root vegetables from Satur Farms on the menu. The connection is hardly coincidental. Chef Eberhard Müller and his wife, Paulette Satur, established Satur Farms on the North Fork in 1997. Their intent was to grow produce for Müller's restaurant. Müller's culinary colleagues in New York City took note of their outstanding results. Now the couple farms full time, providing fresh, local ingredients to top eateries throughout Manhattan and beyond.

The Market Bistro menu offers a satisfying and tasty sampler of Long Island bounty. Among many items, one can choose from local sea scallops, local fluke or Long Island duckling from Crescent Duck Farm in Aquebogue. A curated selection of brews from Long Island's burgeoning craft beer movement rounds out the local menu options.

Market Bistro
519 North Broadway
Jericho, NY, 11753
516-513-1487
marketbistroli.com

Roots Bistro Gourmand

Chefs Philippe Corbet and James Orlandi of Roots Bistro Gourmand have a deep respect for culinary tradition with a postmodern bent. Their highly inventive dishes are rooted in the fundamentals of French cuisine, and they are infused with cutting-edge gastronomic techniques. Dining at Roots suggests a roadmap for what the future of Long Island food might be.

In the past, the one-hundred-year-old West Islip structure housed everything from a speakeasy to a teahouse. The clean, efficient décor is a blend of sophisticated bistro style and rustic farmhouse charm. Corbet hails from the French Alps, was trained at Michelin-starred restaurants and was executive chef at Bouley. Orlandi is a Long Island native who studied at the Institute for Culinary Education in New York, trained at Jean George's and worked as

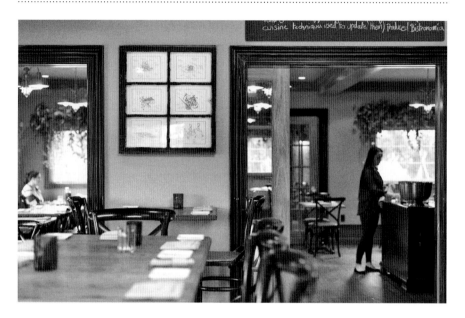

Roots Bistro Gourmand in West Islip serves entrées using traditional and modern techniques in a relaxed setting. *Photo by Jacob Skoglund.*

Corbet's sous chef at O's Food & Wine Bar. The team opened Roots in 2012, inviting patrons to experience a new kind of culinary journey.

Roots entrées are towering, sumptuous creations with layers of flavor, color and texture. The team embraces elements of art and science in their cooking. Corbet "designs" an entrée by sketching the dish in a black composition notebook. Orlandi loves to experiment, applying the latest trends in molecular gastronomy. Entrées are dressed with frothy foams, intensely flavored gels, verdant micro-greens and chef-created Technicolor coulis. "We definitely have a distinctive artistic style," said Orlandi.

The menu is inspired by the seasons. Tender octopus is surrounded by a sea of flavor—artichoke heart, walnut, heart of palm, charred eggplant puree, piquillo-tomato gel and goat cheese panna cotta. A traditional pork belly sandwich is transformed into a work of edible pop art with layers of toasted brioche, pickled red onion and cucumber, a brilliant sunny-yellow house-made mustard, dollops of Swiss cheese coulis and ham gel and sprinkled with crunchy potato popcorn. Classic steak tartare becomes an abstract expressionist landscape that features a deep golden egg yolk atop a ring of aged Gouda panna cotta splashed with black squid ink. There's always a touch of drama in the presentation. For dessert, a chocolate egg tiramisu dissolves into a creamy molten delight under a thin stream of warm chocolate sauce.

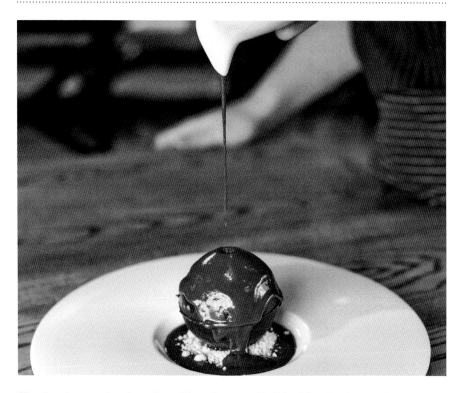

The chocolate egg tiramisu at Roots Bistro Gourmand in West Islip. *Photo by Jacob Skoglund.*

From the outset, Corbet and Orlandi looked to the local community for fresh ingredients. While local sourcing is sometimes seen as a modern culinary affectation, Orlandi said that it is a standard practice long associated with traditional restaurants.

"They walked outside," he explained. "If they didn't grow it, they had nothing. Now we're kind of going back to that." He added that sourcing has become easier, and they work with producers located within a two-hundred-mile radius. The chefs rely on local farms and foragers, and they are expanding their selection of Long Island wines. They are thrilled to have access to fresh snails raised in Peconic that eliminate the reliance on the canned variety. They work with Crescent Duck, the last remaining duck farm on Long Island, and source their oysters from an underwater farm located in West Islip. "I'm five miles away from where I get my oysters," said Orlandi. "I would put this oyster up against any of the best oysters in the world. The salt content and everything in it is just unbelievable."

Food artisans and producers are now contacting them to build relationships that can lead to customization and collaboration on

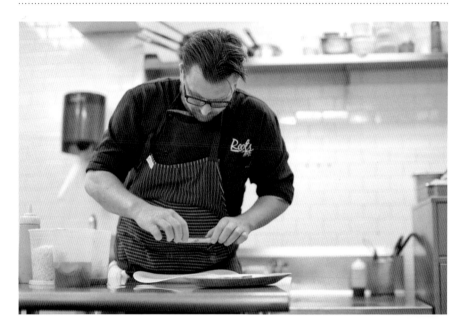

Chef Philippe Corbet preps the pressed pork belly chulo at Roots Bistro Gourmand. *Photo by Jacob Skoglund.*

ingredients and menu items. Orlandi talks of partnering with Koppert Cress to develop micro-greens that are just the right color, flavor and shape for the aesthetic of a unique Roots entrée. Craft brewers are keen to collaborate and create customized beers to serve at the restaurant.

Corbet and Orlandi have just begun to tap the potential for collaboration with Long Island producers, but the ingredients are there. With respect for tradition, high creativity, a commitment to local sourcing and collaboration with producers, Corbet and Orlandi are exploring a new journey for Roots patrons and a new narrative of connectivity for the future of Long Island food. "I guess that's what history is all about," said Orlandi. "It's understanding that historical aspect, but it's also about moving forward and where we're going to bring it in the future."

Roots Bistro Gourmand
399 Montauk Highway
West Islip, NY, 11795
631-587-2844
rootsbistrogourmand.com

Epilogue

Long Island Food

The Common Ingredient

S o, ultimately, how does one define Long Island food? We're not known for a single indigenous food or ingredient. You can't characterize Long Island food as one unique dish or style of cooking. We like to slap a label on food products but don't often think much about the backstory or what it means: Blue Point Oysters, Long Island wine, Long Island duckling, Long Island potatoes. Are any of these labels sufficient to tell the whole story and really capture the flavor of what Long Island food is all about?

Long Island is a vast mix of cultures, traditions and experiences. We grow, prepare and eat a little bit of everything. It's duckling and potatoes. It's pickles and turkey. It's micro-greens and hydroponic lettuce. It's heirlooms, oysters and craft spirits. For some, it's bagels and pizza. And depending on the decade in which you grew up, it's even Dairy Barns and TV dinners.

Can one thing be defined as a little bit of everything? When thinking about food, history can inform our view, as can our understanding of the physical characteristics of a place, the people and their collective experiences.

Food on its own has very little meaning. It's just organic matter. Food takes on meaning when someone plants a seed deliberately, lights a fire, prepares a meal or puts their personal stamp on a food product.

The *aha* moment comes for me when I'm sitting and talking with Karen Catapano alongside her prized goats on a brilliant spring day in Peconic. It is a gorgeous farm and herd that she works tirelessly to maintain, and her exquisite Catapano Goat Cheese is a beautiful product emblematic of her caring nature, her human spirit and her passion for the North Fork.

And that's the answer. That's what Long Island food is about. It's Jacob Ockers creating a business that brings world acclaim to the Blue Point Oyster and Chris Quartuccio reviving oyster farming in the Great South Bay.

It's butcher Peter Zorn building a life for his family in America through a business that his granddaughter Merrill now carries forward.

It's cheese maker Art Ludlow looking for a creative way to reinvigorate his historic family farm.

It's Louisa and Alex Hargrave, determined to cultivate European wine grapes in a former potato field and spawning a nascent wine region.

It's Caroline Fanning and Dan Holmes restoring the land surrounding the Joshua Powell homestead to feed a new generation.

It's Carol and Martin Sidor giving new life to Long Island potatoes.

It's Kassata Bollman connecting city people to country farmers and the food they produce.

It's Nick Voulgaris III caring enough to save Kerber's Farm.

It's master distiller Rich Stabile crafting spirits that conjure up the essence of the home that he loves.

In the end, Long Island food is deeply personal. It's about self-expression. We cultivate and create food that reflects who we are at any given time or place. So if you want to get to know Long Island food, get to know the people who produce it. That's the common ingredient.

Bibliography

Agnew, Meaghan. "A Brief History of Long Island Duck Farming, Before It's Gone." *Modern Farmer* (December 5, 2014).

Agricultural Society of Queens, Nassau and Suffolk Counties. *2014 Long Island Fair Premium Book*. Nassau County, NY: self-published mailer, June 2014.

All American Hamburger Drive-In. http://allamericanhamburgerli.com.

Al-Muslim, Aisha. "Historic Grossmann's Farm Opens for Season." *Newsday* (April 30, 2011).

Barritt, T.W. "Duck Island Bread Company." "Edible Long Island," Winter 2014. www.ediblelongisland.com.

———. "Freeport's Nautical Mile: The Surge After Sandy." "Edible Long Island," October 30, 2013. www.ediblelongisland.com.

———. "The Jericho Cider Mill and Crispen and Idared Apples." "Culinary Types," November 27, 2011. http://culinarytypes.blogspot.com.

———. "Local Food and a Relationship Delivered to Your Door." "Edible Long Island," May 20, 2013. www.ediblelongisland.com.

———. "A Proclivity for Pickles." "Edible Long Island," September 10, 2013. www.ediblelongisland.com.

———. "The Shack in Centerport." "Edible Long Island," July 23, 2013. www.ediblelongisland.com.

———. "Simply Cider and Apples at the Jericho Cider Mill." "Edible Long Island," September 18, 2013. www.ediblelongisland.com.

Bayard Cutting Arboretum. www.bayardcuttingarboretum.com.

Bigar, Sylvie. "Local Fishermen Challenge Our Relationship with Food." *Hamptons* magazine (July 3, 2014). www.hamptons-magazine.com.

The Big Cheese. www.thebigcheeseny.com.

Bigelow's. www.bigelows-rvc.com.

Bleyer, Bill. "LI Maritime Museum's Sloop *Priscilla* Ready for Public." *Newsday* (May 15, 2010).

Blue Duck Bakery Café. http://www.blueduckbakerycafe.com/bakery.

Blue Island Oyster Company. www.blueislandoyster.com.

Blue Point Brewing Company. www.bluepointbrewing.com.

Boody, Peter. "Cheese, Where Potatoes Grew." *New York Times*, September 14, 2003.

Bookbinder, Bernie. *Long Island: People and Places Past and Present.* New York: Harry N. Abrams, 1983.

Brady, Ralph F. *Landmarks & Historic Sites of Long Island.* Charleston, SC: The History Press, 2012.

Browder's Birds. http://browdersbirds.com.

Caruso, Victoria. "'Tis the Season at the Milleridge." *25A Magazine* (December 2, 2013).

Catapano Dairy Farm. http://catapanodairyfarm.com.

Civiletti, Denise. "Blue Duck Bakery Café's Keith Kouris Named One of Top 10 Artisan Bread Bakers in North America." *Riverhead Local*, March 10, 2015.

Crescent Duck Farm. "Our History." www.crescentduck.com.

Dairy Barn Store Inc. "The History of Dairy Barn." www.dairybarn.com.

DiNapoli, Thomas P. "Agriculture by the Numbers: New York Farming Is Big Business." Office of the State Comptroller, August 2012.

Discover Long Island. www.discoverlongisland.com.

Dock to Dish. www.docktodish.com.

Duck Island Bread Company. www.duckislandbreadcompany.com.

East Islip Historical Society. "Bayard Cutting Estate." http://www.eastislip.org.

Entenmann's Direct. "Entenmann's History." https://www.entenmannsdirect.com/history.cfm.

Farmingdale-Bethpage Historical Society. "The Bethpage Purchase." www.fbhsli.org.

Farm2Kitchen Long Island. http://www.farm2kitchenlongisland.com.

Fischler, Marcelle S. "A Couple Find Their Dream in the Field." *New York Times*, December 2, 2007.

———. "Long Island Journal; North Fork Duck Farmer Holds His Ground." *New York Times*, December 6, 1998.

———. "The Uncertain Fate of Farmland." *New York Times*, April 19, 2012.

Freedman, Mitchel. "LI Farm Bureau's First Female President Breaks New Ground." *Newsday* (November 13, 2013).

Gebhard, Glenn. *A Farm Picture: The Life and Times of Long Island Farms.* Distributed by Cinema Guild, 2003.

Georgio's Coffee Roasters. www.georgioscoffee.com.

Gianotti, Peter, and Joan Remick. "Long Island Restaurants that Have Endured for 20-Plus Years." *Newsday* (updated April 25, 2015).

Governor of New York. "Governer Cuomo Marks One-Year Anniversary of Signing the Farm Cidery Law." October 17, 2014. http://www.governor.ny.gov.

Grossman, Karl. "Suffolk Closeup: Hail the Long Island Duck." *Shelter Island Reporter*, May 3, 2015.

Hammond, Gary R. *The Mineola Fair: Mirror of a Country's Growth*. N.p.: self-published, 1999.

Hargrave, Lousia Thomas. *The Vineyard*. New York: Penguin Books, 2004.

Heritage Bakers. www.heritagebakers.com.

Hodesh, Jeanne. "Artisans: The Power of Sour." *Edible East End* (September 8, 2009).

Hometown Long Island. Melville, NY: Newsday Inc., 1999.

Horman's Best Pickles. http://hormansbestpickles.com.

Jacobsen, Aileen. "Fowl Weather." *Long Island Pulse* (October 25, 2013).

Jacobsen, Rowen. "Tomahawk (Shinnecock)." The Oyster Guide, December 2, 2010. http://www.oysterguide.com/new-discoveries/tomahawk-shinnecock.

Jedediah Hawkins Inn. http://www.jedediahhawkinsinn.com.

Jericho School District. "In the Beginning." https://web.jerichoschools.org.

Kalypso Greek Yogurt. http://kalypsoyogurt.com.

Kerber's Farm. www.kerbersfarm.com.

Kirchmann, George, and the Historical Society of the Massapequas. *Signs of the Times: Massapequa's Historical Markers*. N.p.: self-published, April 2014.

Kosar, Kevin R. "Hard Cider." *Oxford Encyclopedia of Food and Drink in America*. Vol. 1. Editor in Chief Andrew Smith. New York: Oxford University Press, 2004.

Landor, Lee. "County Completes Sale of Grossmann's Farm." *LI Herald*, February 11, 2010.

Lessing's—A Tradition of Excellence. "About the Hotel at Three Village Inn." http://www.lessings.com.

Loh, Jules. "Long Island Pickle Work Is Part of an Older Past." *Lewiston Evening Journal*, March 24, 1977.

Long Island Fair. http://www.lifair.org.

Long Island Growers Market. http://longislandgrowersmarket.com.

Long Island New York Guide to Hotels, Events, Restaurants, News and More. "About Long Island." www.longisland.com/long-island.

———. "Long Island Roads." www.longisland.com/roads.

———. "Long Island Traffic." www.longisland.com/traffic.

Long Island: Our Story. Melville, NY: Newsday Inc., 1998.

Long Island Potato Festival. "History of Potatoes on Long Island." www.lipotatofest.com.

Long Island Seed Project. www.liseed.org.

Long Island Traditions Inc. http://www.longislandtraditions.org.

Madore, James T. "Suffolk Loses Title as State's Biggest Agriculture Producer." *Newsday* (March 5, 2015).

Malverne Historical & Preservation Society. "History of Malverne Village." http://www.malvernehistory.org.

Marcus, Erica. "Blue Duck Bakery Hits the Big Bread Leagues." *Newsday* (May 3, 2012).

———. "10 Best Things I Ate in 2014." *Newsday* (December 18, 2014).

Market Bistro. http://www.marketbistroli.com.

Miller, Carrie. "And Then There Was One Long Island Duck Farm; Crescent." *Riverhead News-Review* (September 19, 2014).

————. "Could $700K Help Bring 'Ag Center' to Downtown Riverhead?" *Riverhead News-Review* (December 19, 2014).

Milleridge Inn. "The History of Milleridge." http://milleridge.com.

Montalbano, Tom. "The Great Syosset Pickle Boom." *Syosset Stories by Tom Montalbano*. Oyster Bay Historical Society. http://www.oysterbayhistorical. org/syosset-stories.html.

Nassau County. "Old Bethpage Village Restoration." http://www. nassaucountyny.gov.

Newsday. "Time Machine: And It Doesn't Look a Day Over 150." September 12, 1999.

North Fork Potato Chips. http://www.northforkchips.com.

North Fork Sea Salt Company. www.northforkseasaltco.com.

Novick, Susan M. "Jericho; From the Old Millhouse, Cider." *New York Times*, October 8, 2006.

Oak Tree Dairy. www.oaktreedairy.com.

Orkestai Farm. www.orkestaifarm.org.

Oyster Bay Brewing Company. http://oysterbaybrewing.com.

Oyster Festival. http://www.theoysterfestival.org.

Park Connect. "Park-to-Table, a New Way to Connect to State Parks Takes Root." September 2014. http://archive.constantcontact.com/ fs110/1108652353464/archive/1118608856685.html.

Pascal, John. "A Man Who Knows About the Hen." *Newsday* (September 20, 1972).

Peconic Land Trust. "Peconic Land Trust Acquires Conservation Easement of 1.1 Acre Parcel, Part of Historic Farmland on Cobb Road in Water Mill." Press release, May 5, 2011. https://www.peconiclandtrust.org/ pdf/pressreleases/PR_05042011_Halsey_CobbRd.pdf.

Planting Fields Foundation. http://www.plantingfields.org.

Relish. http://www.relishkingspark.com.

Restoration Farm. www.restorationfarm.com.

Richmond Hill Historical Society. "American Indians of Long Island, NY." www.richmondhillhistory.org/indians.

Roots Bistro Gourmand. www.rootsli.com.

Satur Farms. http://www.saturfarms.com.

Sayville Library. "Businesses: West Sayville—Waterfront & Shellfishing." http://sayvillelibrary.org/Waterfront_Shell_Fishing.html.

The Shack. http://www.theshack25a.com.

Shinnecock Indian Nation. www.shinnecocknation.org.

Simply Hydroponics and Organics. "What Is Hydroponics?" www.simplyhydro.com.

Sleter, Greg. "Islip Town Launches Aquaculture Program." *Sayville-Bayport Patch*, March 27, 2011.

Slow Food USA. "Newtown Pippin Apple." www.slowfoodusa.org.

Southold, New York. http://www.southoldtownny.gov.

Sparkling Pointe. http://sparklingpointe.com.

Starkey, Joanne. "A New Rustic Bistro (Comes with a Crowd)." *New York Times*, January 20, 2012.

Stony Brook Village Center. "History of Stony Brook Village." http://www.stonybrookvillage.com/history-of-stony-brook-village-ny.

Suffolk County Government. "Farm Development Rights Program." www.suffolkcountyny.gov.

Taste of Long Island. https://www.atasteoflongislandny.com.

Thera Farms. http://TheraFarms.com.

Town of Oyster Bay, Long Island, New York. "Town History." http://oysterbaytown.com/town-history.

Ulrich, Karen. "Native Aquaculture: Shinnecock Oyster Farms." *Edible East End* (October 11, 2010).

Verbarg, Ronald. *A Brief History of the Eastern Long Island Duck Farm Industry.* Suffolk County Department of Planning, February 2009.

Volpe, Gianna. "North Fork Wineries, Aquebogue Orchard Jump on Cider Trend." *Suffolk Times*, November 22, 2012.

Weitz, Emily J. "Getting the Catch Directly to the Restaurant." *New York Times*, September 5, 2014.

Woodside Orchards. http://woodsideorchards.com.

Zorn, Merrill. "Zorn Family Oral History." Private collection, June 2, 2014.

Zorn's of Bethpage. http://zornsonline.com.

Personal Interviews

Biancavilla, Robert. Northport, New York, September 27, 2014; April 25, 2015.

Bolkas, Teddy. Ronkonkoma, New York, March 28, 2015.

Bollman, Bruce. Greenport, New York, May 1, 2015.

Bollman, Kassata. Telephone interview. Seaford, New York, November 8, 2014.

Bollman, Scott. Telephone interview, New York, New York, November 11, 2014. In person, Greenport, New York, May 1, 2015.

Bull, Priscilla. E-mail interview. New York, New York, March 30, 2015.

Campbell, Jennifer. Great River, New York, September 14, 2014.

Cassin, Mark. Massapequa, New York, February 21, 2015.

Catapano, Karen. Peconic, New York, May 1, 2015.

Cheslock, Kelsey. Southold, New York, February 7, 2015.

Fanning, Caroline. Telephone interview. New York, New York, October 1, 2014.

Gammon, Bob. Aquebogue, New York, February 28, 2015.

Gergela, Joseph. Telephone interview. Seaford, New York, September 11, 2014.

Haim, Gabe. Oyster Bay, New York, December 28, 2014.

Kouris, Keith. Southold, New York, January 17, 2015.

Ludlow, Art. Bridgehampton, New York, May 1, 2015.

Makinajian, Michael. Huntington, New York, April 25, 2015.

Mazard, Nicholas. Cutchogue, New York, February 7, 2015.

Quartuccio, Chris. West Sayville, New York, November 8, 2014.

Raleigh, Maura. Kings Park, New York, February 21, 2015.

Schaefer, Elizabeth. Malverne, New York, September 13, 2014.

Schlotter, Ryan. Oyster Bay, New York, December 28, 2014.

Shalam, David. Syosset, New York, December 7, 2014.

Sidor, Carol. Cutchogue, New York, January 17, 2015.

Stabile, Richard. Telephone interview. New York, New York, January 20, 2015.

Starr, Peter. Hicksville, New York, April 24, 2015.

Staub, Erin. Telephone interview. Seaford, New York, April 2, 2015.

Terry, Ethel. Telephone interview. Seaford, New York, March 29, 2015.

Trastellis, Nicholas. Telephone interview. Lenox, Massachusetts, October 30, 2014.

Vasilas, Alethea. Telephone interview. Seaford, New York, April 2, 2015.

Voulgaris, Nicholas, III. Huntington, New York, September 20, 2014.

Zorn, Merrill. Bethpage, New York, January 10, 2015.

Index

About the Author

T.W. Barritt is a native of Nassau County, Long Island, and he grew up in the heart of suburbia in the 1960s. He has spent his professional career working in broadcast media and communications. Since 2006, he has chronicled the evolution of Long Island's food culture through his blog, "Culinary Types" (culinarytypes.blogspot. com). A highly trained amateur chef, Mr. Barritt attended the French Culinary Institute in New York City and is a regular contributor to the magazines *Edible Long Island* and *Edible East End*. His essays on food history are featured in *Entertaining from Ancient Rome to the Super Bowl*, a two-volume encyclopedia published by Greenwood Press in 2008.

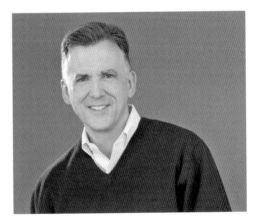

Photo by Ana Miyares.